A Family Life Nature Series

The Gospel
According to a
TREE

By Terry & Jean McComb

Illustrations by Vera McMurdo

TEACH Services, Inc.
P U B L I S H I N G
www.TEACHServices.com • (800) 367-1844

World rights reserved. All national and international rights reserved on the entire contents of this publication.

The author assumes full responsibility for the accuracy of all facts and quotations as cited in this book. The opinions expressed in this book are the author's personal views and interpretations, and do not necessarily reflect those of the publisher.

This book is provided with the understanding that the publisher is not engaged in giving spiritual, legal, medical, or other professional advice. If authoritative advice is needed, the reader should seek the counsel of a competent professional.

All rights reserved. No part of this publication may be reproduced, stored in a retrieval system, or transmitted in any form or by any means, except for brief quotations in printed reviews, without the prior permission of the publisher. Portions of this book may be photocopied for evangelistic purposes.

Copyright © 2023 Terry & Jean McComb
Copyright © 2023 TEACH Services, Inc.
ISBN-13: 978-1-4796-1236-9 (Paperback)
ISBN-13: 978-1-4796-1237-6 (ePub)
Library of Congress Control Number: 2022937747

Any personal website addresses that the author included are managed by the author. TEACH Services is not responsible for the accuracy or permanency of any links.

Scripture taken from the New King James Version®. Copyright © 1982 by Thomas Nelson. Used by permission. All rights reserved. Italics omitted.

Illustrations by Vera McMurdo

Published by

Please Notice Carefully

The book in your hands is a multi-lesson teaching device that will involve the parent, grandparent, or teacher in a family-type activity in God's Outdoor Classroom.

Each page is a stand-alone lesson that is: 1) a reading lesson, 2) a character lesson,

3) a Bible lesson, 4) a science lesson, and 5) an art lesson (color the picture) per page.

Each lesson is created to have the parent/teacher take the child outside and share the lesson by the real object of nature under study. The lesson can be tailored either up or down, based on the child's level of experience and understanding. Later have them carefully color the art opposite the text. The Practical Project accomplished outside will awaken curiosity to desire to know the Creator Who made such a wonderful object of nature.

The art page may be photocopied for classroom use but not for resale.

This resource is excellent for Sunday/Sabbath school use or Boy/Girl Scout Club devotions. VBS leaders will find these lessons very useful. Also, pastors can use these in the children's story time in the worship service. Have the child color the picture while the pastor preaches, thus doubling the attention span of any child.

"God has shown His invisible attributes, His eternal power, and divine nature, clearly by what He has made. People are without an excuse for not glorifying God as Creator and giving Him gratitude and thanks" (Romans 1:20–21, McComb paraphrase).

ENJOY!!

A Word of Thanks

Special thanks to the English class of Fountainview Academy of 1989–90. These classes did some of the original research in this book.

Kathy Sparks, Carla Scarbrough, Twyna Webber, Jennifer Kenney, Pam Dunn, Robbie Dunn, Julie Fournie, Lori Forget and Brian Scarbrough.

Preface

A tree speaks to us of the beauty and wisdom of our Creator. Job 12:8 says: "Speak to the earth and it will teach you." As authors, we have prayerfully pondered the science of trees, then compared them to the ways of God as found in His word. Because God is the Designer and Sustainer of the tree as well as the Author of the Scriptures, we find perfect harmony between the two, one illustrating the other.

Learning about the Creator through what He made was the school attended by Adam and Even in the Garden of Eden. To help them, Adam and Eve were clothed with a perfect light similar to God's (see Psalm 104:3). This light enlightened not only their surroundings but also their mind. Although greatly veiled, God promises enlightenment to His seeking children today (see Revelation 3:13; Ephesians 5:13).

It is the authors' hope that parents and teachers will take the lessons in this book and share them at their child's level of understanding, in the out-of-doors classroom. The drawings used are scientifically accurate and are intended to be colored by the child after completing the lesson.

As you read and experience the living messages from the tree, we pray you will indeed find them to be as leaves from the TREE OF LIFE.

VERA MC MURDO, Artist

Vera and her husband Rex made their home in Whitefish, Montana. Vera was famous for her oil paintings of train steam engines. She was the mother of two boys, Reggie and Martin.

She had never created a line drawing till she began *The Gospel According to Nature* series. She told me she was not interested in money, but in a ministry for boys and girls, so they could know Jesus Christ as Creator.

Vera worked on this project for five years part time, and it became her last labor of love. In 1997 she was diagnosed with cancer and struggled to complete this series of drawings. Her last picture was the picture depicting the tree of knowledge of good and evil, which she never quite finished.

Vera passed to her rest September 28, 1998. How appropriate are the words of Revelation 14:13, "Then I heard a voice from heaven saying to me, 'Write; "Blessed are the dead who die in the Lord from now on."' 'Yes,' says the Spirit, 'That they may rest from their labors, and their works follow them.'"

She did not live to see the last two books she illustrated published. How pleased she will be resurrection morning to meet all the boys and girls who were blessed by her art ministry. This book is lovingly dedicated to her memory.

Table of Contents

Page	Nature Object	Bible Text	Character Lesson
4	Preface		
6	Tree Factory	Genesis 1:26	Service
8	Roots	Ephesians 3:17	Abuse
10	Bark	Psalm 119:63	Protection of Friends
12	Xylem and Phloem Cells	Proverbs 3:19	Wisdom
14	Sap	Psalm 104:16	Good for Evil
16	Rings of a Tree	Ecclesiastes 12:13, 14	Habit
18	Limbs	Psalm 55:22; John 1:9	Heavy Burdens
20	Branches	John 15:5	Honor Parents
22	Buds	Isaiah 6:11	Patience
24	Leaves	Matthew 5:48	Carefulness
26	Tree Flowers	Genesis 1:12	Reproduction
28	Fruits of a Tree	Matthew 7:20	Influence
30	Seeds	Galatians 6:7, 8	Cause & Effect
32	Coniferous & Deciduous Trees	Psalm 1:3	Love
34	Green vs. Dry	1 John 5:12	Respect for Life
36	Growth	Jeremiah 17:7, 8	Growth
38	Thinning	Romans 12:2	Individuality
40	Forest Community	Ephesians 6:4	Sharing
42	Atmosphere	1 Corinthians 10:31	Attitude
44	Tree House	Psalm 84:3	Protection
46	Tree Values	Psalm 139	Talents
48	Tree Music	Isaiah 55:12	Listening
50	In the Rain	Isaiah 55:10, 11	Relaxation
52	Tree Memories	Luke 22:39, 40	Private Devotions
54	Cedar of Lebanon	Psalm 92:12–15	Security
56	Tree of Good and Evil	Joshua 24:15	Alertness
58	Wounds and Diseases	Isaiah 53:5	Forgiveness
60	Death of a Tree	Romans 6:11, 23	Self-denial
62	Four Seasons	Ecclesiastes 12:1	Aging
64	Tree of Life	Revelation 22:2	Immortality
66	Appendix A	Theory of Sap Movement	Curiosity
68	Bibliography		
70	The Gospel According to Creation Seminars		

Tree Factory

Trees have been called living fountains of life gushing out of the earth, then falling into a billion droplets of green leaves. Some loggers say the cottonwood tree, when cut down, will ooze water for several days from its stump. This describes why a tree could be called a wooden pump with a pipeline deep down into the earth, pulling the hidden moisture up to add its vapor to the dry air. Its natural products are pure air and humidity, edible fruits and nuts, wood for man and other creatures. Besides all this, each part of the tree ministers to some other part of the tree. The opposite page illustrates the entire manufacturing process found in a tree, from root to leaf.

Each process reveals the principle of the cross—the law of self-denial. This principle is seen in everything God created except the selfish heart of man. You will find it demonstrated on nearly every page of this book. This principle was clearly made known to the universe when God's Son Jesus Christ died to save one little world that went astray.

The tree and the human family both testify they have the same author. Here we see evidence of a Divine Designer who put it all together. God's Word was right when He said of trees: 'it was good' in Genesis 1:12, "And the earth brought forth...the tree that yields fruit, whose seed is in itself according to its kind. And God saw that it was good." Yet the human family is infinitely more complicated than a tree. Genesis 1:27 says, "So God created man in His own image: in the image of God He created him; male and female He created them."

The history of a family has been referred to as a family tree. The children are the branches, Mom and Dad the trunk of the tree. Then there are the roots, the grandpas and grandmas and great grandpas and great grandmas, and on, until we finally get back to Adam, who "was the Son of God" (Luke 3:38). The final root stock of the family tree ends up with God. Not some slime, black hole, explosion, or evolution, but God. "For this reason I bow my knees to the Father of our Lord Jesus Christ, from whom the whole family in heaven and earth is named" (Ephesians 3:14, 15).

PRACTICAL PROJECT

Draw your family tree and compare it to a real tree.
What are the services Mom and Dad render to their children?
What do the limbs, the children, do for the family?
What do they do for society around them, by way of service?
Try to trace your family tree back three or four generations, perhaps even with photos.

Tree Factory

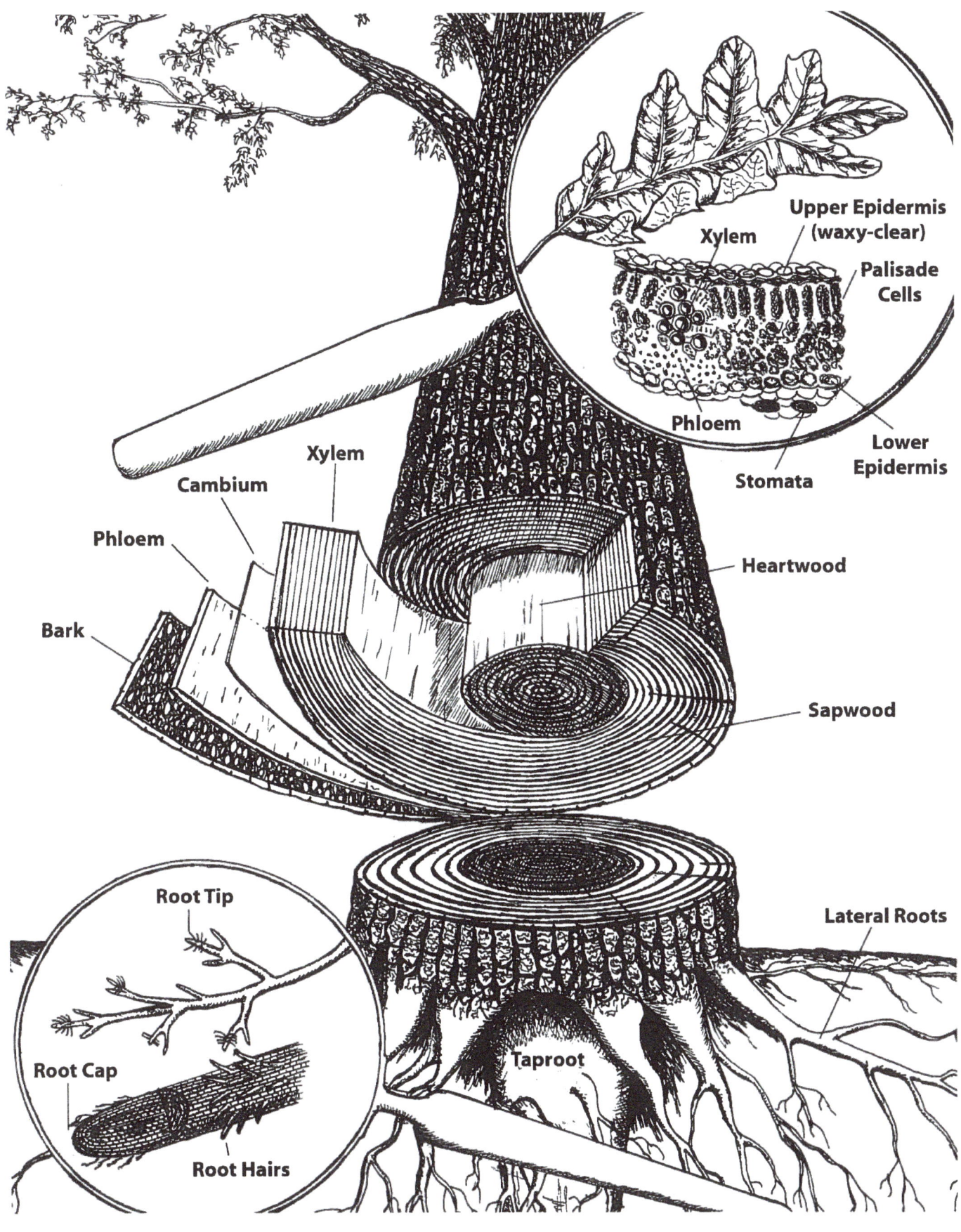

Roots

A large healthy tree has as much root underground as it has branches above ground. The giant sequoia has a root system that extends over two or three acres. Roots are the tree's foundation and anchor. It is not a beautiful part. Here, hidden out of sight, the tree receives moisture and nourishment, and some trees store it. This part of the tree enables it to live through famine and drought which kills other plants with a smaller root system. Likewise, memorized Scripture acts like an anchor holding one stable through difficult times.

Edwin Markham, a famous nineteenth century poet, said, "When the great oak is straining in the wind, the boughs drink in new beauty, and the trunk sends down a deeper root on the windward side." Trees, too close together, have a shallow root system and can blow over easily. When spaced further apart, they put down a large root system. As the wind blows, they grow stronger.

On a mountaintop we see trees that grow stunted from harsh conditions. Children living with criticism may receive a message that behavior is more important than they are. Little roots of bitterness spring up. (See Hebrews 12:15.) If parents sink their roots deeper on the windward side into the Saviour's love (see Ephesians 3:17), passing on to their children God's grace with loving limits, all can grow stronger when the winds of trouble blow.

The only place where roots grow and absorb nutrients and water is at the very tip. Here tiny root hairs act like little straws, absorbing whatever is around them. As they grow, they give off carbon dioxide gas which combines with water in the soil to form a weak acid, carbonic acid. This acid dissolves the minerals in the soil and enables the root tips to absorb them.

In a similar way, we absorb God's word and memorize or store it out of sight.

Caution! The same active faith that absorbs promises, can as easily absorb bitterness. Each day brings new absorption, new growth. Yesterday's experience will not do for today's growth. What we absorb depends where we are rooted: in the love of God or self.

Underneath a tree lies great mysteries: How do rootlets find water? What gives them wisdom to grow in that direction? We may never know. Here are divine mysteries. How God's love transforms our hearts is a similar mystery.

PRACTICAL PROJECT

Take radish seeds and place them in a napkin soaked in warm water. In three days, the seeds will sprout and become covered with tiny fuzzy hairs. Watch how much water they can absorb. How many promises can you absorb from God's Word that will help root you in God's love and enable you to face the strong winds of life? To memorize a passage easier: First day read 25 times; Second day read 20 times; Third day read 15 times; Fourth day read 10 times; Fifth read 5 times; by the sixth day it should be memorized.

Roots

"That you, being rooted and grounded in love, may be able to comprehend with all the saints what is the width, and length and depth and height – to know the love of Christ which passes knowledge; that you may be filled with all the fullness of God" Ephesians 3:17-19.

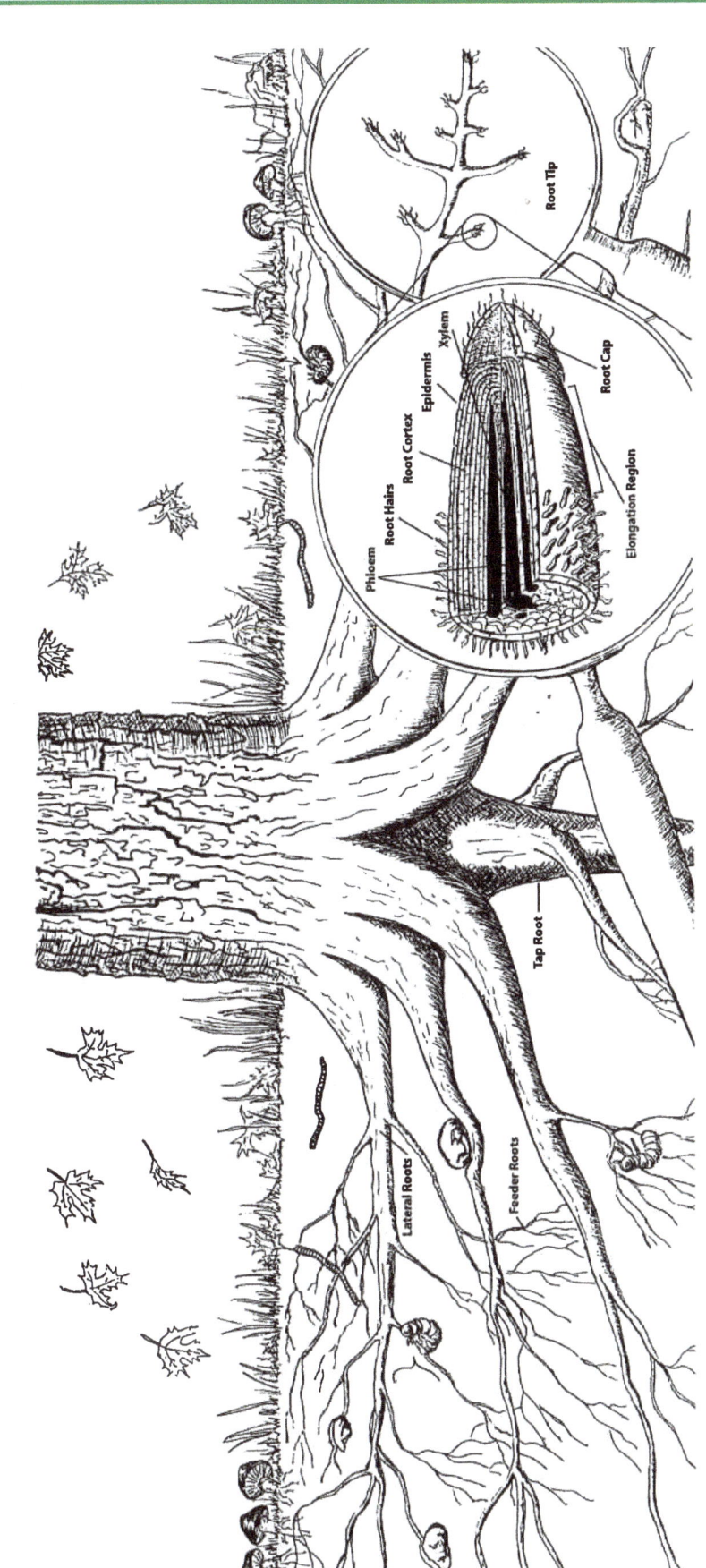

These root hairs grow only on new growth. The past growth becomes tough, hard and waterproof. Thus new growth is essential to a tree's life.

So with our life. Yesterday's growth is history; hard and unchangeable. Only today's growth flexes, changes, and absorbs. Tomorrow is future unknown. We can only LIVE today.

Bark

Tree bark functions similarly to human skin. This outside barrier protects the tree against invasion of insects, pests, and disease. The bark also functions similarly to clothing, insulating and beautifying.

As the phloem cells bring nutrients down from the leaves, these cells eventually harden and become part of the bark. Just as your fingerprint can identify who you are, so can a tree be identified by looking closely at its bark. In like manner, divine truths stored in the mind become habituated thought patterns in your life, protecting and identifying you as the bark protects and identifies the tree. "Stand therefore having girded your waist with truth" (Ephesians 6:14).

When young people love those best who love Christ most, it becomes a very deep protection. During the three years I was at a high school boarding academy, no one ever offered me a girlie magazine or invited me to a movie, or offered me a cigarette, drugs, or alcohol, or told dirty stories around me. Why? I openly declared Jesus and His followers as my best friends and to the best of my ability walked in harmony with His word. Psalm 119:63 says: "I am a companion of all who fear You, and of those who keep Your precepts." I choose those who love Christ most for friends.

With Jesus as my best friend, His presence by the Holy Spirit said "No" to a thousand temptations. I did not need to say "No," for the divine Holy Spirit "bark" protection, already said "No" for me.

We gain many products from the tree bark: rubber is tapped from the bark of a rubber tree; cork from the cork tree bark; cinnamon from the bark of certain trees of the laurel family; quinine from the bark of a South American tree. The active agent in aspirin is from the willow tree bark. Bark grows from the inside out as all true Christians grow: "My son, give me your heart, and let your eyes observe my ways" (Proverbs 23:26). Tree bark with its unique beauty, protection, and healing, is a fit illustration of what Jesus wants to do for us from the inside out.

PRACTICAL PROJECT

Go for a walk in the woods. Practice identifying trees by their bark. Try this blindfolded. You can do this in spring, summer, fall, or winter for the bark of a tree is the same in any season. An individual's external dress, fashion, hairstyle, and make-up are similar to the bark of a tree. As a family go to a mall and watch people go to and fro. By their external dress or undress, can you identify the friends of the world and the friends of Jesus? (Study James 4:4–10.) Who are we seeking to become best friends with: the world or Jesus? Love those best that love Christ most. Did Jesus become "the friend of publicans and sinners" by dressing, looking, and acting like sinners, or did He offer them something better?

Bark

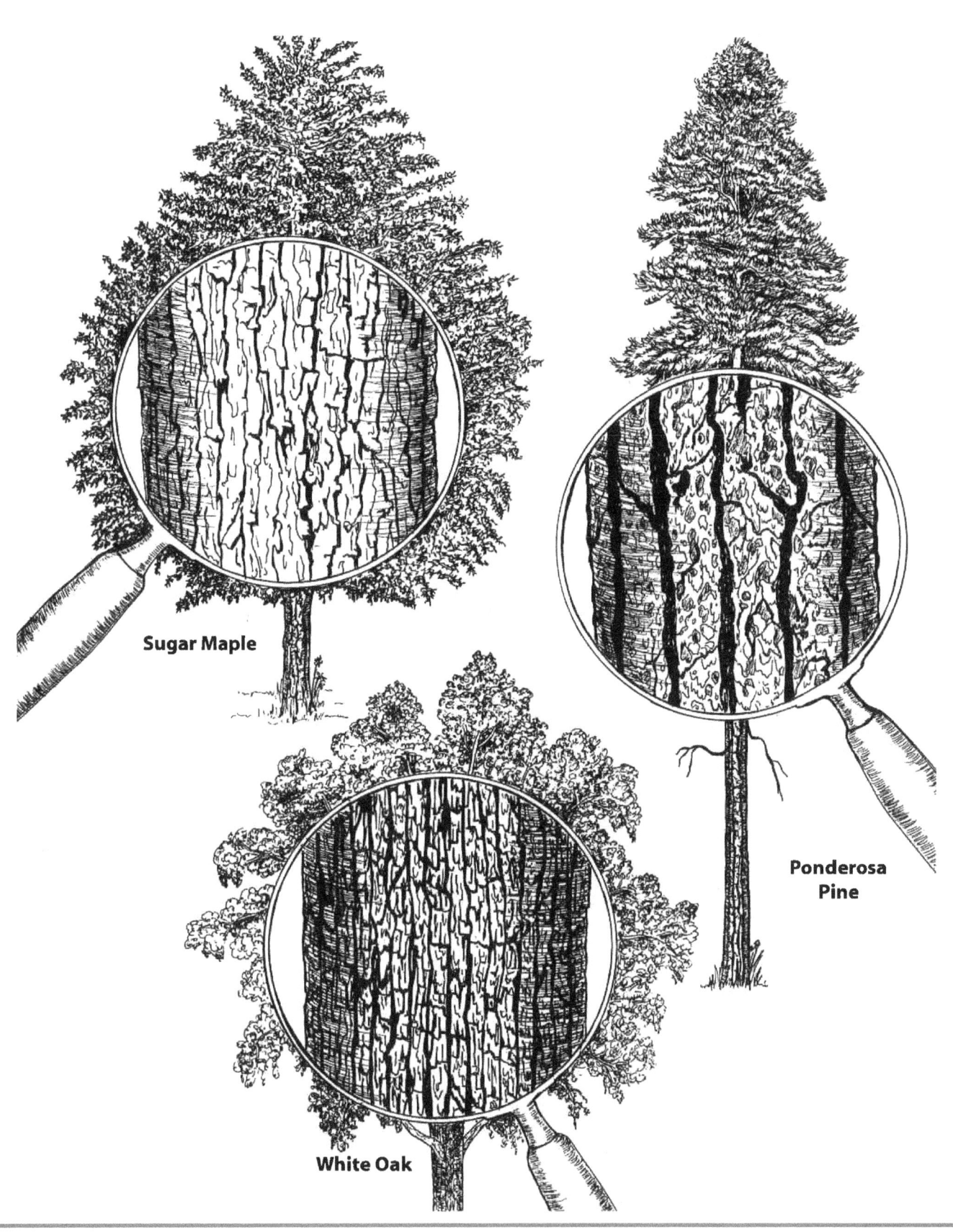

# Xylem and Phloem Cells

How does sap go up a tree? To answer this question needs more than the wisest science of man. Proverbs 3:19 tells us, "The Lord by wisdom founded the earth; by understanding He established the heavens."

The opposite page shows us an image of pine tree xylem ducts. The secret of how sap goes up a tree still eludes modern science. Why are there little concave disc-like holes in the xylem cell? What function do they play as sap goes up the tree to the leaf?

These xylem cells eventually will become clogged with sap and will become part of the sapwood and eventually heartwood of the tree. These xylem cells are all manufactured by the one cell thick cambium layer, and they cover the tree from the twig to the root.

When the cells of the cambium layer divide, they produce on the inside of the cambium layer xylem cells—with perfect little holes such as you see in the picture. On the outside of the cambium layer it will produce phloem cells which take the sugars and saps manufactured in the leaf back down to the root. (see picture from chapter 1) How does this one cell thick cambium layer function which to make—cells taking fluid up or cells taking fluid down?

How does this cell have engineering technology to produce perfect little circles? Every little circle says, "Made by God." Try drawing one circle without the aid of a compass and make it perfect, and then draw three more the same size, without a compass. Circles are only one of the awesome creative skills revealed in the production of these transportation cells. We are looking at the mechanics and structure of some kind of a pump. As far as we can see, there are no visible moving parts. We know this action can lift fluids 300 feet high. How does the cell lift fluids? There are many hypotheses, but none have been widely accepted by the scientific community.

The phloem cells are made quite differently. These are hollow tubes containing screen-like sieves. How do they work? These carry the sap down, the opposite direction of xylem cells, which carry the sap up. How does the tree make decisions? Does it use some kind of electrical energy? No one knows. All these mysteries cause us to simply bow our heads in gratitude and say: "...Worship Him who made heaven and earth, the sea and springs of water" (Revelation 14:7).

(See Appendix A on sap movement.)

 ## PRACTICAL PROJECT

Take 3 different kinds of wood: Oak, Maple, and Pine and compare them.

Notice their differences. They are all xylem cells. Even when these cells die, they have many uses for us as wood. So with you and me. We too were designed for many different uses, but we can all bring glory to our Creator.

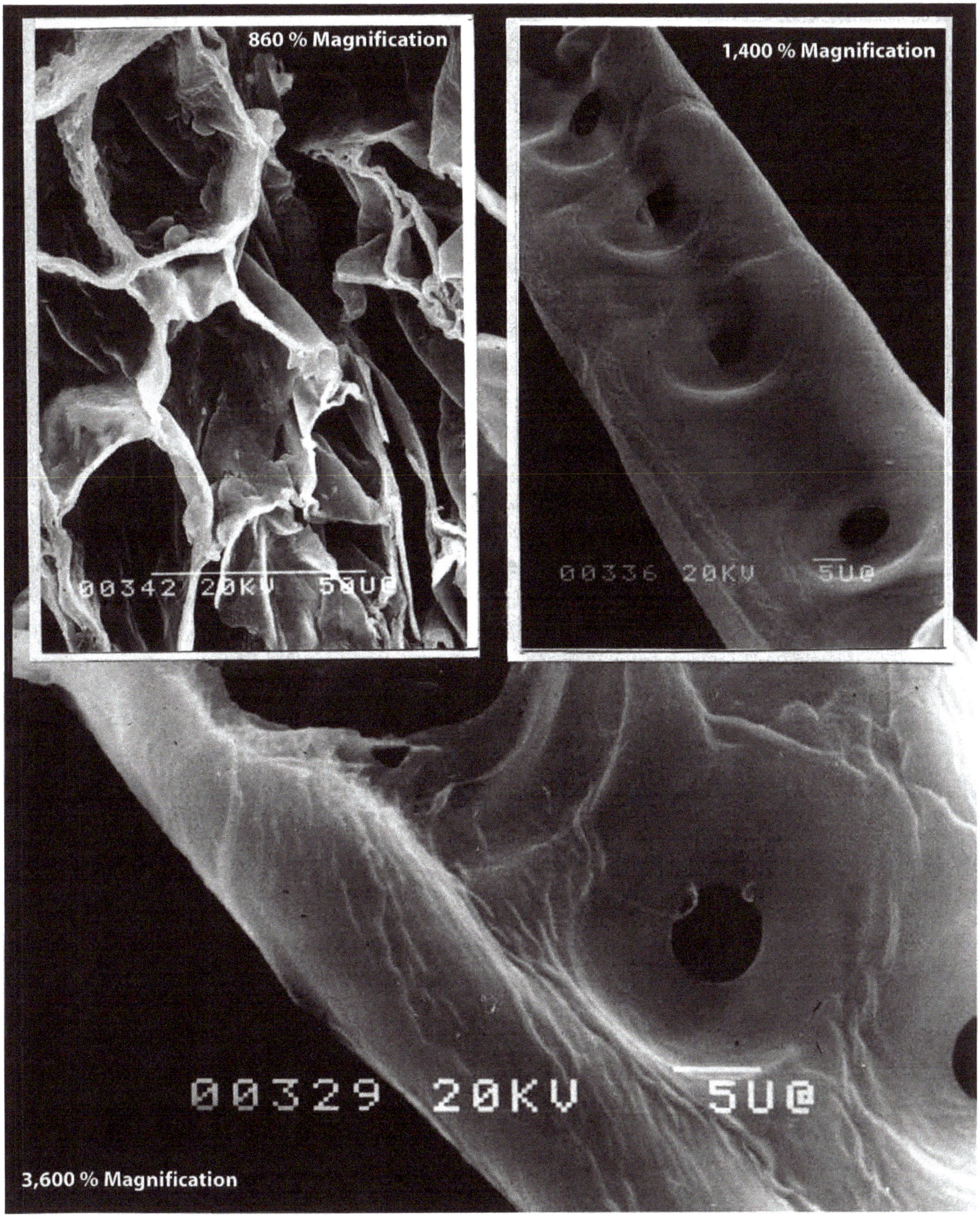
860 % Magnification
00342 20KV 50U@
1,400 % Magnification
00336 20KV 5U@
00329 20KV 5U@
3,600 % Magnification

micrographs by David McComb

Sap

The whole life of the tree centers in that one little word: sap—a colorless liquid, looking very much like water. Sap contains all that ministers to the life of a tree.

The leaves manufacture sap. The phloem and xylem cells transport it to every living cell of the tree, and the roots also store it. Delicious maple syrup is made from the sugar maple sap. This is collected as shown on the opposite picture.

When the nights are cold and the days are warm, a tree may yield a hundred drops of sap a minute per drilled hole. This liquid is so full of water that 40 gallons of sap must be boiled down to make one gallon of maple syrup. Similarly, a most delicious provision Jesus has made available to us is His love. He took all the love of the centuries and boiled it down to three and a half years of ministry. This love climaxed at the cross in an ultimate demonstration of self-denial.

In sap are found all the elements necessary for new growth, for maintenance, and for healing. Sap is to the tree what blood is to the human body. Sap vividly demonstrates the incredible ability God has put in nature to repair damage and to compensate for losses. Different trees have different saps, depending on the needs of the tree.

Rubber is made from the sap-like latex that oozes out when the rubber tree is cut. Another sap product known to man is turpentine, which is made from pine-tree sap. In Psalm 104:16 we are likened to trees full of sap. "The trees of the Lord are full of sap." It is God's plan that those who have this sap, will be able to respond to cuts and mistreatment the same way He did. 1 John 3:16 says, "By this we know love, because He laid down His life for us. And we also ought to lay down our lives for the brethren."

PRACTICAL PROJECT

With help from an adult, in Spring, drill a small hole in a maple or birch tree. See if you can observe the sap coming out.

Find sap on a variety of trees that formed from an injury. Notice the differences.

Years ago, children used sap that was gummy for chewing gum.

Family thought: When we are hurt by others, what comes out of our mouths?

What comes out of our mouth comes from our heart. Is my heart born again or is it just fallen human nature?

When Jesus died on the cross He shed His (sap) blood for you and me. Blood is to our life what sap is to a tree. When Jesus is crowned Lord of my life, He brings divine love with His humanity. My humanity united to His blood humanity links us to His divinity. John 17:26 can then be experienced at home, school, work, church-anytime, anywhere. Even when hurt! "That the love wherewith thou hast loved me may be in them, and I in them." Imagine. . . divine love to share with not a thread of selfishness! This is sweetness every home needs.

Sap

Rings of a Tree

As a sapling grows, cell by cell, a tree ring is formed. Every drop of rain, every ray of sunshine is recorded on the growth rings. Each has its part in making up the heartwood of a tree. Likewise, day after day you lay down a series of thoughts and deeds that produce rings of character. Each is unerringly written upon the mind. Together they make up your character, a walking bundle of habits.

One can count the years of a tree by counting all the dark rings, or all the light rings. Do not count both. Trees lay down a dark ring and a light ring each year. Start in the center, the rings are further apart. As you move towards the outside, the rings are closer together. You may need to use a magnifying glass because the rings are so close together. The growth rings in a tree are like a birthday candle—one for each year.

The rings in a tree are made during two times of major growth: spring and summer. Spring growth is light in color because the xylem vessels carry large amounts of sap. The summer growth is darker because the xylem vessels are smaller.

In a similar way, a child will grow and learn more in the first seven years of life than in all the rest. In the adolescent and adult years, the growth is slower and more difficult than in the first seven years. The two growth rings make up the grain of the wood and when stained, absorb the stain differently, thus enhancing the beauty.

How important becomes the admonition of Scripture, "Whether you eat or drink, or whatever you do, do all to the glory of God" (1 Corinthians 10:31). Every habit counts. Soon in the judgment when the annual growth rings of our life are examined, Jesus will be looking for how His Word was absorbed and lived. "Remember now thy Creator in the days of thy youth…" Why? "Let us hear the conclusion of the whole matter: Fear God, and keep his commandments, for this is the whole duty of man. For God shall bring every work into judgment, with every secret thing, whether it be good, or whether it be evil" (Ecclesiastes 12:13, 14). It is all recorded upon the nerve endings of our minds as surely and accurately as the growth rings are recorded in the heartwood of a tree.

🌿 PRACTICAL PROJECT

Find a tree's age by counting the number of rings in a tree stump like the one on the opposite page. What kind of seasons has it lived through? Make a diary of the tree by noting the width of its rings. Which tell of bounteous years, and which of lean?

Which tell of the healing of wounds, of new heights gained and kept? Keep a diary of habits you are forming.

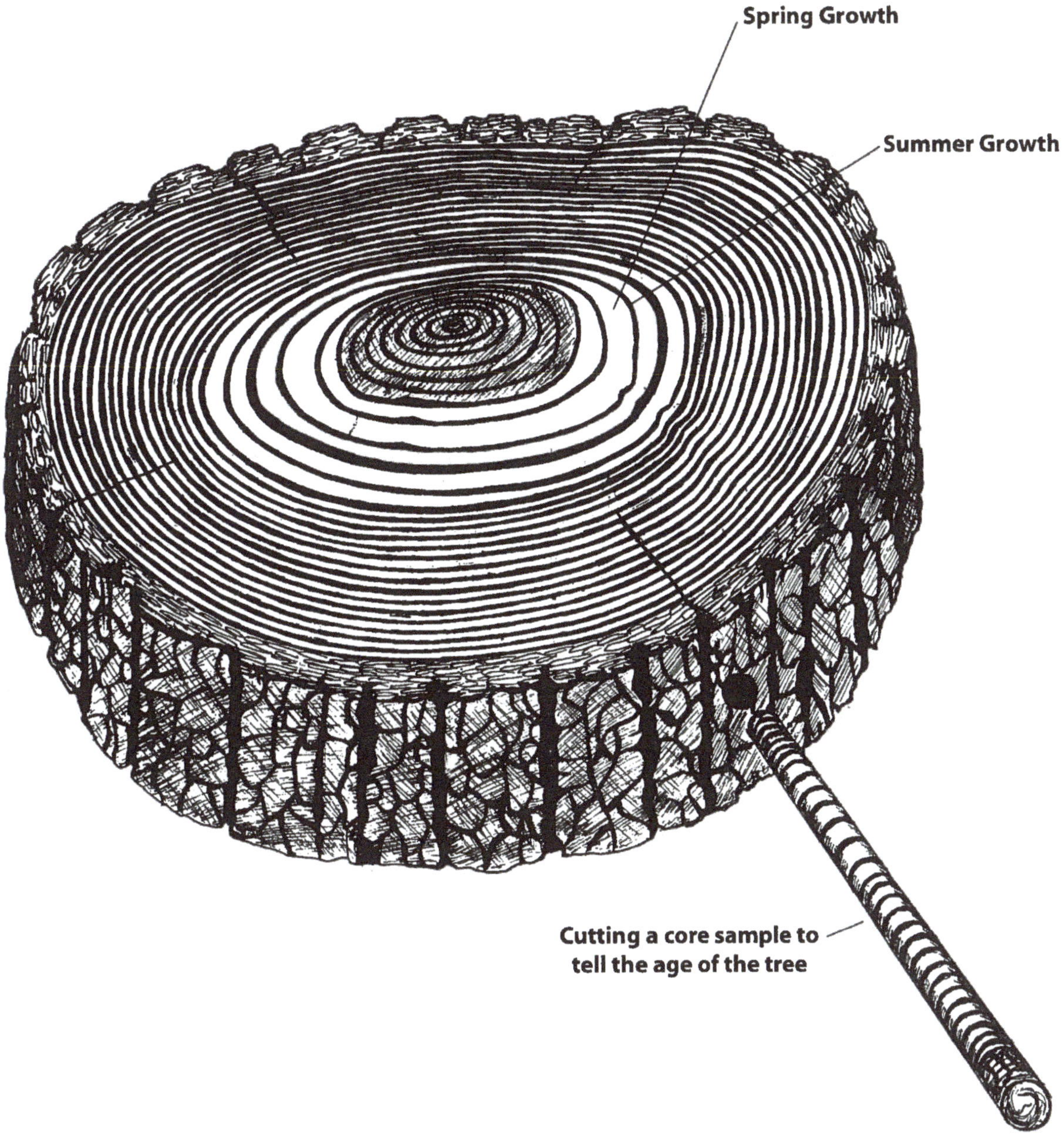

Rings of a Tree

Spring Growth

Summer Growth

Cutting a core sample to tell the age of the tree

Limbs

When sticky snow falls heavily, the limbs begin to sag. The more the white blessings hold on, the more the limbs bend under the weight. Weak limbs often snap under the load. In mercy the wind scatters these accumulated blessings. When scattered, the limbs spring back to their uplifted positions, offering praise to their Maker. Solomon said, "There is a time to get, and a time to lose; a time to keep, and a time to cast away" (Ecclesiastes 3:6).

So with us, when given a birthday cake, pass the excess blessing on before one sags and bags with excess calories. Pass blessings on to the less fortunate before wind, pain, and disease force one to let go. Sometimes the wind of strife, in reality, is the love of our Father freeing us from too many accumulated blessings.

Often parents appear like a tree heavily laden with snow—the dishes to be washed, the house to be cleaned, the garbage to be emptied—all burdens God did not intend parents to carry alone. Children can carry a small portion of the load on their limbs of the family tree. All are called to "endure hardships as a good soldier of Jesus Christ" (2 Timothy 2:3). Children who are willing to bear burdens, to take the hard place, to do the work that needs to be done, are preparing to carry successfully their own adult burdens one day.

The heaviest burden on our tree, whether old or young, is the burden of sin. To tell a lie, to injure a friend and not make it right, are burdens too heavy to bear. John 1:9 says, "If we confess our sins, he is faithful and just to forgive us for our sins and to cleanse us from all unrighteousness." Christ will carry our burdens when we give them to Him. He has prepared a way of release. Psalm 55:22 says, "Cast thy burden upon the Lord, and He will sustain you." He will carry every load.

PRACTICAL PROJECT

After a heavy snowfall, go out into the yard and find some limbs bowed down with snow.

Notice how heavy their load. Take the end of a limb and try to lift it up.
Are you able to bear the same weight as the limb?
How heavy is the load on the limb?
Try holding your arms out from your body, like a tree.
How long can you hold your arms out?
Experiment: Try this for a sweet night of sleep. Before bedtime have a clearing conscience time. Confess the sins of the day so all can go to sleep with all burdens of sin forgiven and cleansed by Jesus, the burden bearer. Does it help you have a sweeter night's sleep?

Limbs

Branches

A branch is not the tree, but it is like a miniature tree. The branch often looks like the tree, only it grows sideways instead of up and down. In this case, the tree branch is rooted and grounded in the tree itself. How is a limb fastened to the tree? What glue holds it there? What is the source of its strength? The branch receives water and vitality from the tree. The tree receives sugars and manufactured energies from the leaves through the branches back to the tree.

As you look at some trees, you will notice that the limbs higher up on the tree grow almost straight up, and as you move down the tree, they get bigger, longer, and curve, until gradually gravity pulls them closer to the ground. It is almost as if the tree is pointing heavenward in a position of prayer and praise—the attitude we need in order to be alert and alive.

Each year the tree adds a layer of life, adding a layer to the branch also; thus, its strength is acquired from many layers of spring and summer xylem cells. All branches keep on branching, getting smaller and smaller, until finally the limb ends and there we find a bud. All this branching is so the food manufactured in the leaf may be effectively transported back to the tree by the phloem cells and down to the roots where it will be available to the tree for use now and later.

The branch depends on the tree for its total support. So it is with us and Christ. Jesus said in John 15:5, "I am the vine, you are the branches. He who abides in me, and I in him, bears much fruit; for without me you can do nothing." All the growth of the limb depends upon what it receives from the tree. Likewise, any fruit we bear depends upon what we receive from Christ. The key word is abide—a living connection of our humanity with His divinity.

In a similar way, children are like limbs on the family tree. To a great degree, all comes via the genetics of father and mother. Children are a miniature extension of the family tree. When we honor our parents, we are honoring the name that we took from them. What we are on the inside will eventually bring either glory or shame to the family name.

"Honor your father and mother, that your days may be long upon the land which the Lord your God is giving you" (Exodus 20:12).

 PRACTICAL PROJECT

Take a sheet of paper and try sketching a tree. Sketch a branch.
How many times did it branch or divide?
Is it haphazard?
Is there a pattern to the branching?
Does the tree minister to the life of the branch or does the branch minister to the life of the tree?
Do children minister to the family tree or does the family tree minister to the children?
How is it in your family?

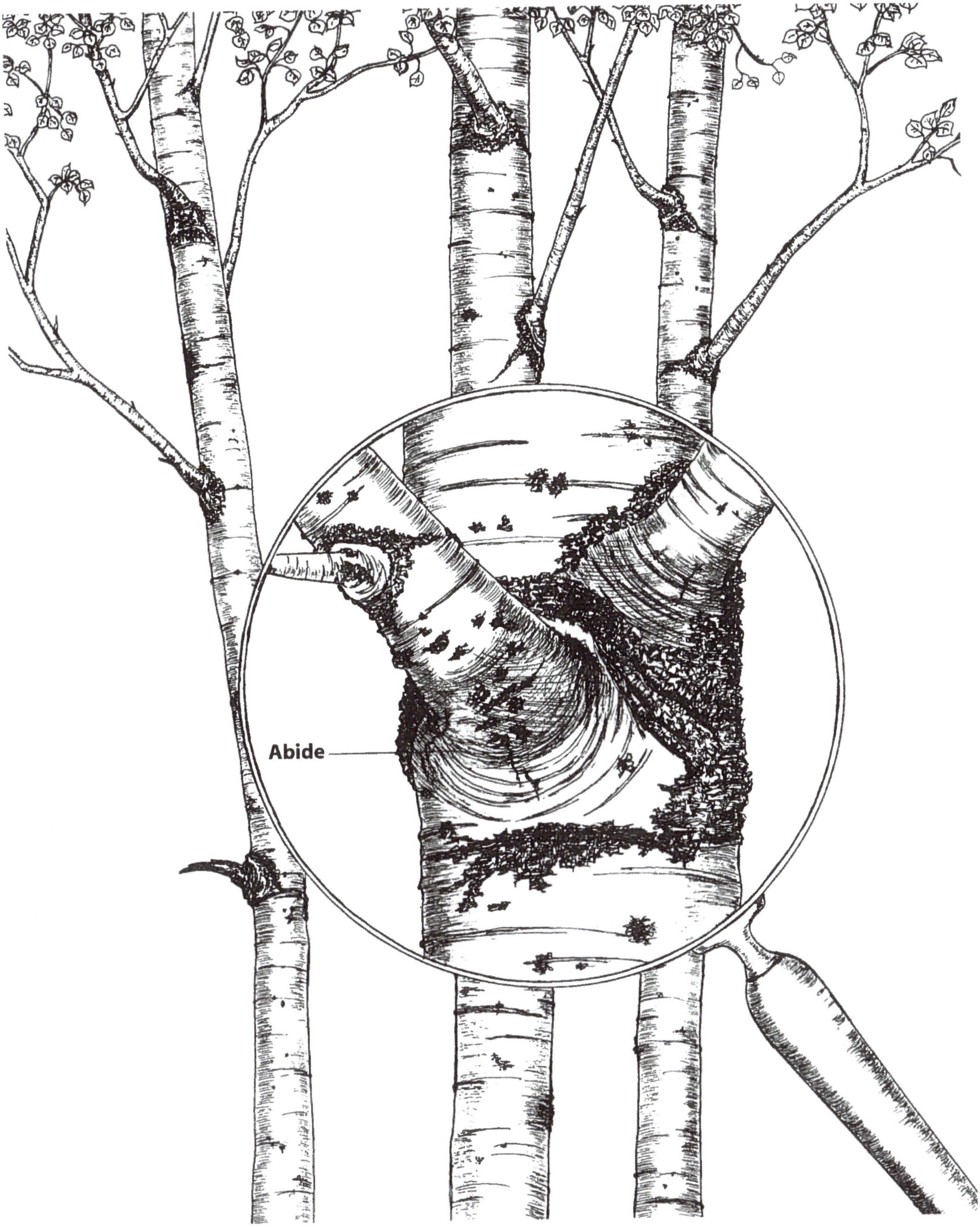

Branches

Abide

21

Buds

Buds are baby leaves. We think of them as opening in the Springtime, but they actually begin to grow one year earlier. The tree gives very careful attention to the buds, for they are indeed the future life of the tree. The picture on the opposite page is a birch tree. Its buds grow all summer while the tree has the resources needed for their development. In autumn, when the leaves fall, the buds are already prepared for next spring, but they still remain carefully wrapped, tucked away, and protected in their winter coats.

If you open a bud you will discover they are very tightly compacted. They are the epitome of maximum use of space. God has carefully put around these buds something like antifreeze, enabling them not to freeze, yet the antifreeze is non-toxic to the plant itself.

Trees have their own birthday candles. You can tell how old a limb is by counting the bud scar rings. Notice the bud scar ring near the end of the branch on the opposite page. Above the scar ring is this year's growth. Count down from that ring to the next lower ring, and you will know how much that limb grew in the past year. By counting the bud scar rings, you will know the age of the limb.

Isaiah 61:11 says, "For as the earth brings forth its bud, and the garden causes the things that are in it to spring forth, so the Lord God will cause righteousness and praise to spring forth before all the nations."

Children are often anxious to grow up fast before they have the self-control to handle the choices they have to make. Buds, however, have a full year's growth, sleeping through the winter preparing to burst forth the following spring. Similarly, self-control and righteousness are like a bud. They take a long time to develop according to God's timetable. Maturity takes time. Being rooted and grounded in Christ will indeed cause self-control and righteousness to spring forth. But if the bud is forced open too early, it is greatly marred, if not destroyed.

PRACTICAL PROJECT

An interesting and challenging activity is to find the keys to identify winter trees by their buds.

Pick several different twigs with buds. Place them in different cups of water with food coloring added—one red, one blue and one yellow. As they grow, watch the leaf color change according to the color of the water. What spiritual lesson can you learn from that experiment?

Go for a walk as a family and see if you can count the bud ring scars and tell the age of the limb.

Try opening a bud too early. Can you help it grow faster?

Buds

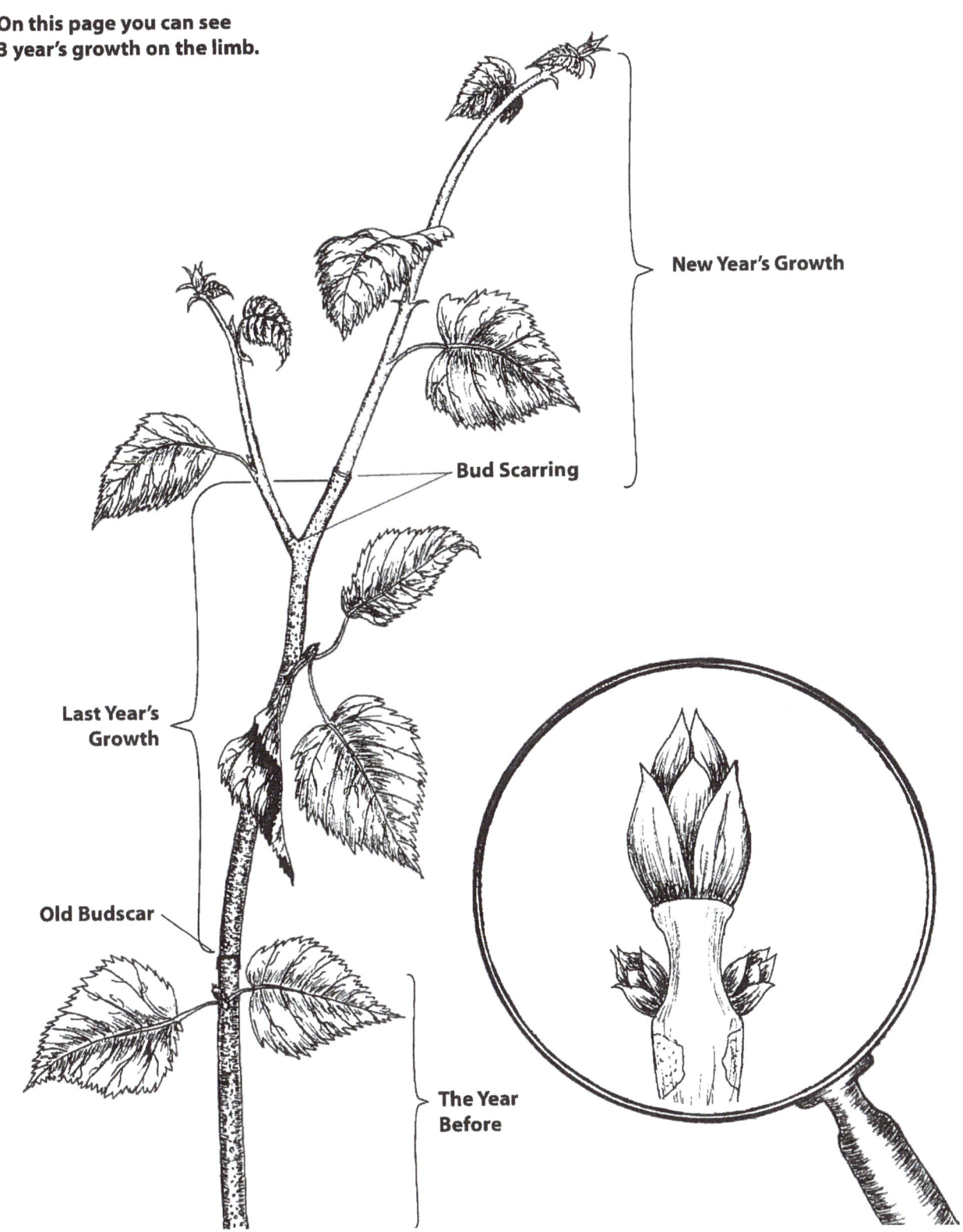

On this page you can see 3 year's growth on the limb.

New Year's Growth

Bud Scarring

Last Year's Growth

Old Budscar

The Year Before

23

Leaves

Leaves are the key maintainer of the life of a tree. Without leaves a tree will die. A leaf is really the chemical laboratory of the tree. We can picture it as the tree's heart, mouth, lungs, stomach, digestion, intestines, nervous system, and hormonal system.

On the opposite page take a close look inside the leaf beginning at the bottom left magnifying glass. Note the delicate plumbing of the xylem and phloem cells that transport sap to and from the leaf. This plumbing leads us to Step One: the leaf takes in water and sap. Step two: the leaf takes in carbon dioxide through the breathing pores or stomata. Step three: the leaf takes in energy from the sun via palisade cells. Step four: the leaf gives away pure oxygen and excess water via the stomata. Step five: this photosynthesis (light process) takes place in the upper right magnifying glass. The chloroplast smash open the carbon dioxide, take the carbon out and transform it into carbohydrates-glucose sugar. The sugars, fat and protein are then passed on to the tree to be stored in the roots, or to make fruit or to be used as energy for the life of the tree. The tree in this process gives away 80% of the water it took in from the roots out its breathing pores. No man-made lab can duplicate this process.

This exchange can be made only in a living cell. Only life can create life. Here is a true unsolved mystery. Don't remove the mystery from science. "These are mere edges of His ways, and how small a whisper we hear of Him!" (Job 26:14).

The higher the magnification, the more clearly we read in fine print the words, "Made by God." All this complex engineering is used only one season, and then it is thrown away. The whole process starts over next spring with a new laboratory!

A leaf reveals God's love of perfection. "Be perfect, just as your Father in heaven is perfect" (Matthew 5:48). Like the leaf, we should strive in our sphere to represent God's perfection, by allowing Him to work out through us the principles of His Holy Word: justice, mercy, and goodness. These may be demonstrated in the first relationships ever formed in life—the child/mother/father relationships.

Nothing is too small for our Heavenly Father's care or attention. On every leaf His name is written. We can fully trust ourselves in His care.

PRACTICAL PROJECT

With a pocket magnifying glass hold a leaf up to the sunlight and see if you can find any of the items on the opposite page. Vacuole; stomata (or mouth, usually on the bottom side of the leaf); and chloroplasts. This little leaf factory works faithfully for the tree and it works for you and me. What jobs are we to do today? How can we be more faithful with them?

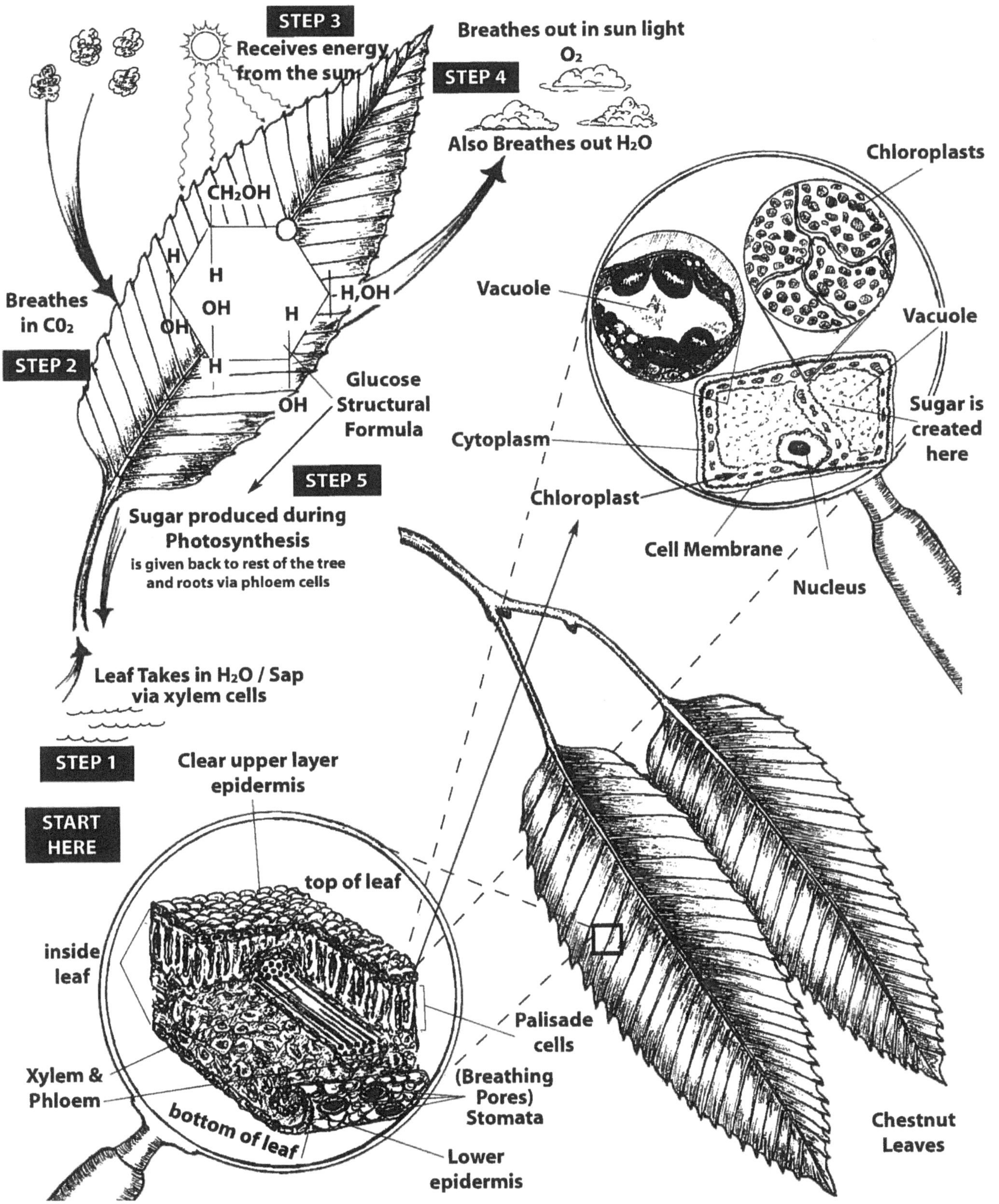
STEP 3
Receives energy from the sun
Breathes out in sun light
O_2
STEP 4
Also Breathes out H_2O
CH_2OH
H
H
OH
H
H,OH
OH
H
OH
Breathes in CO_2
STEP 2
Glucose Structural Formula
STEP 5
Sugar produced during Photosynthesis
is given back to rest of the tree and roots via phloem cells
Leaf Takes in H_2O / Sap via xylem cells
STEP 1
START HERE
Clear upper layer epidermis
top of leaf
inside leaf
Xylem & Phloem
bottom of leaf
Palisade cells
(Breathing Pores) Stomata
Lower epidermis
Chloroplasts
Vacuole
Vacuole
Sugar is created here
Cytoplasm
Chloroplast
Cell Membrane
Nucleus
Chestnut Leaves

Tree Flowers

All parts of a tree work together for one common goal, flowers. All trees have flowers. On some trees the flower is not very visible because it is an incomplete flower. A complete flower has all four parts: 1. sepals, 2. petals, 3. stamens (male parts), and 4. pistils (female parts). The crabapple tree has a complete flower.

Many trees have incomplete flowers—they don't have both pistils and stamens, making it a single sex flower. These are pollinated by the wind. A large tree group such as birches and poplars bear catkins. Catkins either produce male pollen or female ovule but never both. In other trees, the male and female flowers may be on the same tree, but separate. Such is the case of beech trees. Cottonwood and holly trees have a separate male and female tree.

Conifer trees are cone bearing and I call the cone a type of flower, although in strictest scientific terms they are classified differently from a flowering tree. They function like a flower. The female cone and male bearing cone look like a funny type of flower. All flowers have one great purpose—reproducing its 'kind' by way of seeds. In Genesis 1:12 we read, "the tree that yields fruit, whose seed is in itself, according to its kind: and God saw that it was good." On this third day of creation God created the parent plant with seeds 'after its kind.'

Darwin's theory of evolution is a complete failure, when considering reproduction. By themselves, the ovule (the female egg) and pollen (the male part) have no future. Only when the two unite will the cycle be completed and a new seed formed. If we "evolved" one flower with both male and female parts, there could be no second flower without an insect to carry the pollen to the female part. Evolution teaches insects evolved millions of years after the flowers! The way insects, flowers, and wind work together to accomplish reproduction almost surpasses belief. Inspiration declares: "And God saw that it was good" (Genesis 1:12).

Children are the seed of a family. Father is the male part, mother the female part. Both unite with God in the creation of new life in a baby. That makes every human being on planet earth a child of God. "Love your neighbor as yourself" (see Matthew 19:19) for all are children of the Creator. All have been given this gift of life. Treasure it and pass it on with holy reverence.

PRACTICAL PROJECT

Go for a walk and see if you can find the flowers of a tree, its seeds, or both.

See if you can identify the male part (stamen) and female part (pistil). You may need a more detailed book from the public library for the specific tree's flowers to make positive identification of the flower parts.

Tree Flowers

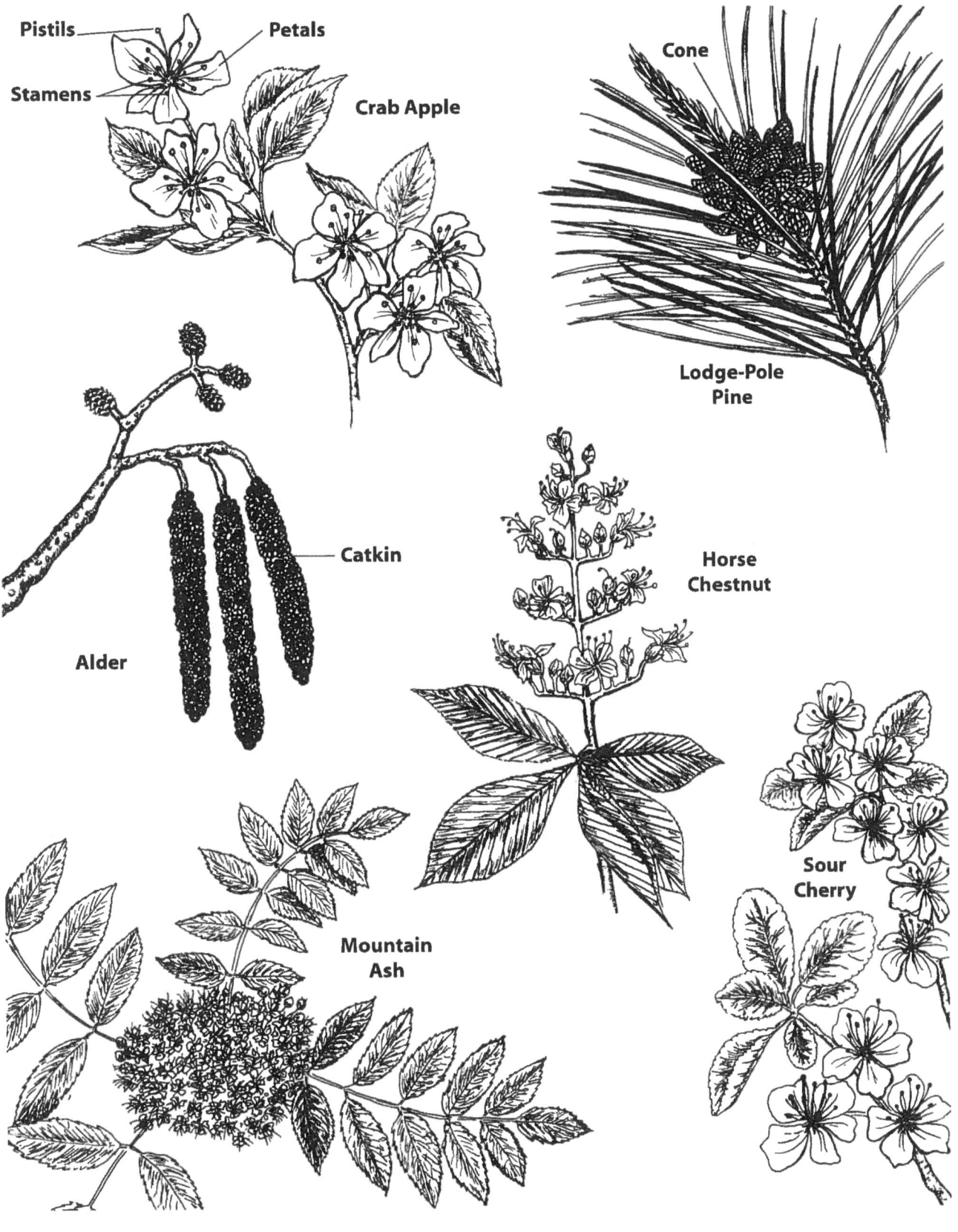

Fruits of a Tree

All of the fruit on the opposite page have one thing in common: they contain seeds. Biology defines fruit as that "part of a flowering plant that contains the plant's seeds." The fruit testifies of the character of the tree's seeds. A plum tree bears plum fruit. A crab apple bears crab apples.

Every elementary boy or girl can understand that fact; but a harder truth to learn is: "Even so every good tree bears good fruit, but every bad tree bears bad fruit. Therefore by their fruits you shall know them" (Matthew 7:23). Wise is that boy or girl who loves those best who love Christ most.

When a child eats an apple, in reality the apple is a gift from God just as much as if God were to place the apple in his or her hand. Without the on-going commands of God, the apple tree would die, "for without Me you can do nothing" (John 15:5). Daily He bestows life-giving properties on all that nature produces, including fruits and its seeds.

Fruit bearing is very important. Jesus came to a fig tree that had leaves. This unique tree starts growing fruit before it puts out leaves. When Jesus found nothing but leaves, the tree was cursed and cast off. Christ is looking for divine fruit, the fruit of His own life. Jesus said, "Abide in Me and I in you. As a branch cannot bear fruit of itself, except it abides in the vine, neither can you except you abide in Me" (John 15:4).

So, the principle is clear. If we abide in Jesus, we will bear His divine fruit. If we simply abide in self and remain selfish and carnal, then we will bear crab apple fruit. Let us guard carefully our influence. Those who are around us—mother, father, brother, sister, classmates—observe us. As they sample our words, deeds, attitudes, and thoughts, let them see revealed Christ's "seed" from within.

PRACTICAL PROJECT

Take the seeds from an apple or an orange, and plant them in a paper cup.

Give them soil and moisture and sunshine and watch them grow. Thus, we can see the cause and effect of the seed. They reproduce the kind of seed from which they come.

What seeds are you partaking of and what kind of fruits are you bearing on your tree of life?

(Compare fruits of the Spirit with fruits of the flesh in Galatians 5:19–22).

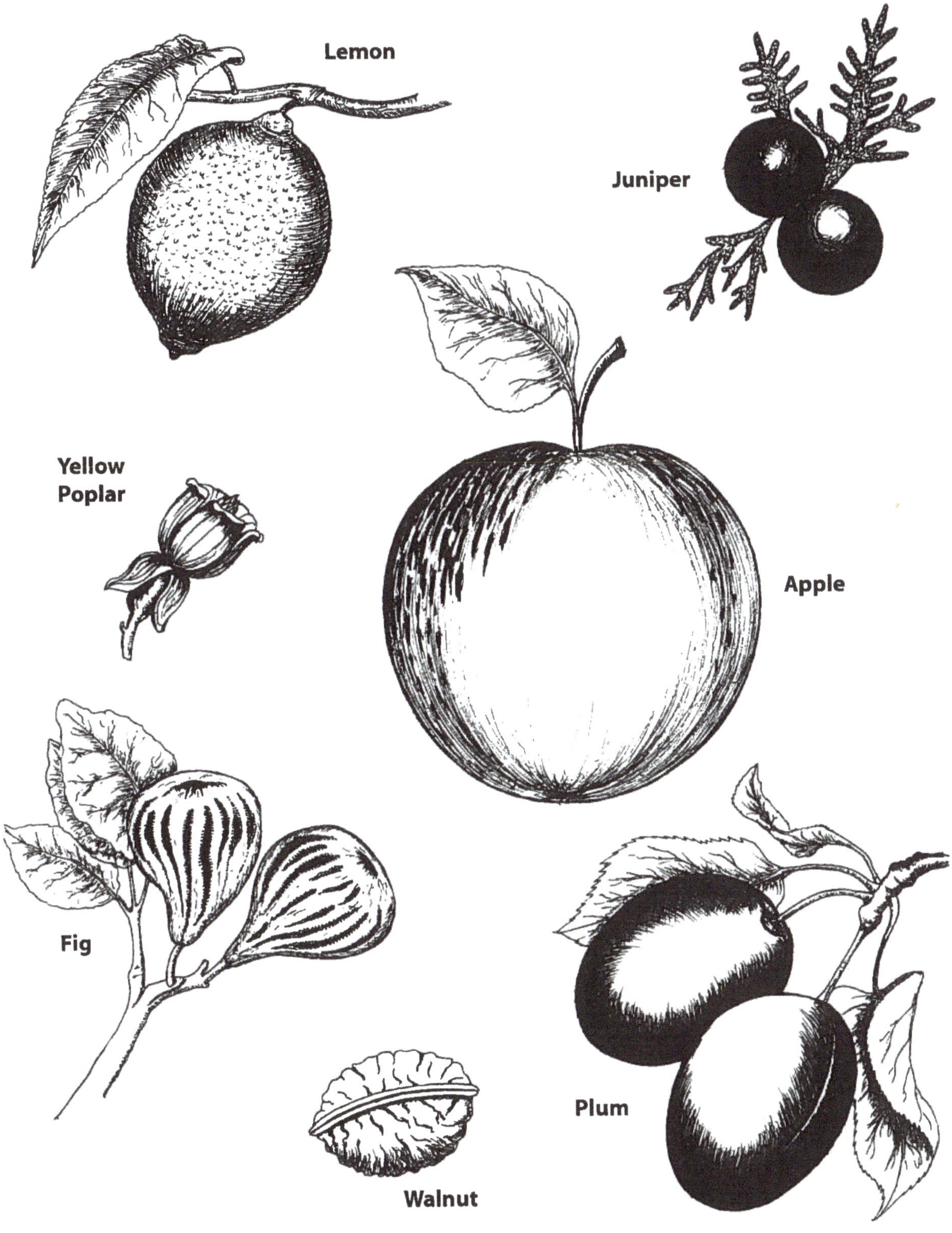

Fruits of a Tree

- Lemon
- Juniper
- Yellow Poplar
- Apple
- Fig
- Walnut
- Plum

Seeds

An awesome force in the world of nature is growth. A good example of that force is seen in seeds of the giant sequoia. This seed is so small that it takes 3,000 seeds to weigh one ounce. Here the law of multiplication is beyond belief. This tiny flaky seed has grown for some 35 centuries and is still growing, reaching a height of over 300 feet and measuring some 40 feet in diameter. All these tons of tree vegetation actually come from that tiny flake of seed! We gaze at the giant Sequoia Redwoods, and marvel—all that from a tiny seed!

There is a promise in 2 Corinthians 9:10 that promises this kind of unbelievable growth in our lives. It works upon the principle of multiplication. It holds hope for His children who will receive His seed, be it ever so tiny. "Now may He who supplies seed to the sower, and bread for food, supply and multiply the seed you have sown and increase the fruits of your righteousness" (2 Corinthians 9:10). "The seed is the word of God" (Luke 8:11).

The outside layer of a seed is a protective coat. Underneath this coat lays the embryo or living part of the seed. The embryo contains the blueprint for the stem, leaves, and root. About 15% of all seeds actually have vitality enough to sprout. Perhaps one seed out of one million will actually sprout. Before many sprout, they are attacked by squirrels and jays. So with us, many things try to choke out the seed of God's Word in our daily life.

The seed that sprouts reproduces the parent plant. Galatians 6:7, 8 shares this law, "Do not be deceived, God is not mocked: for whatever a man sows, that he will also reap. For he who sows to his flesh will of the flesh reap corruption, but he who sows to the Spirit will of the Spirit reap everlasting life." Fallen human nature can receive divine seed through the "Seed Catalog"—His Word! When planted in the soil of our minds, that seed can grow and multiply, even as a seed weighing one three thousandth of an ounce can become a giant sequoia.

 PRACTICAL PROJECT

Find a pinecone and put it in a warm place to dry. When dry take the seeds out, and plant them in a paper cup by a window and see how many of them actually grow.

Seeds

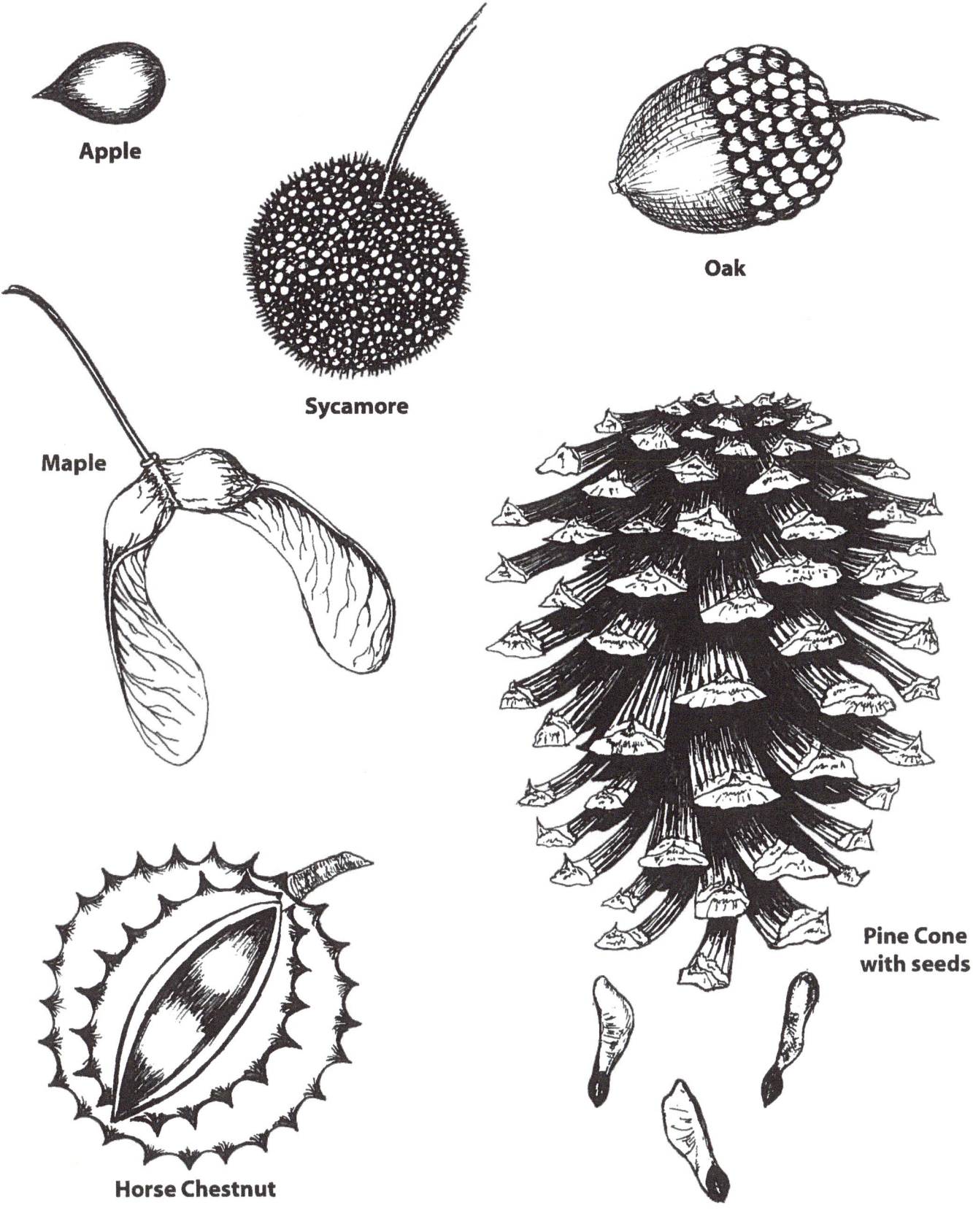

Coniferous & Deciduous Trees

There are two basic types of trees that live in our world.

1. **Deciduous trees**, including many broad-leafed trees and also a few conifers that shed their needles in fall, and 2. **Evergreen trees**, that do not shed their leaves all at the same time, including many conifers and some broadleaf trees too.

In summer, the enchanting forest is clothed in a mantle of living green. When fall winds blow away the colorful yellow and reds, leaving stark, bare limbs on the deciduous trees, then the evergreens stand out! In a similar way, people can all look the same, but those who are rooted and grounded in Christ, who walk in humility, distrustful of self, clinging, even trembling to the hand of Christ, will reveal their true character when times become cold or rough. When subjected to the storm of trial, the truly righteous (those whose natures are being transformed by the divine nature of Christ), will wear the robe of Christ's righteousness in prosperity and adversity alike.

The conifers also have a particular pine-oil odor, a fragrance that broad-leafed trees do not normally have. There are health-giving, life-giving properties in these conifer forests. Likewise, those who are rooted and grounded in Christ, will give off a special fragrance unlike any other, "a sweet-smelling aroma, an acceptable sacrifice, well pleasing to God" (Philippians 4:18) that tells of a source of life outside themselves.

The oldest living thing known to man is the bristle cone pine, residing in the high Sierras of California. This tree began to grow shortly after the flood waters receded from the flood of Noah's day. It is now well over 4,000 years old. Generation after generation have lived and died. The Prince of Peace, the Lord of Life, Jesus Christ came, lived, and even died on a tree, then He arose, and still this tree continues to live. Today this tree, still has life. It reminds us of the wonderful promise in Psalms, "He shall be like a tree planted by the rivers of water, that brings forth its fruit in its season, whose leaf also shall not wither, and whatever he does shall prosper" (Psalm 1:3). The "He" in this verse is the one who meditates day and night on God's law, and is "ever-green."

🍃 PRACTICAL PROJECT

Go for a walk in the forest as a family, sit down in the shade of an evergreen, and pick the bough of an evergreen and one of the deciduous tree and note the similarities rather than the differences. How is it with your family? In times of trials and difficulty, are you evergreen, full of the life and love of Christ?

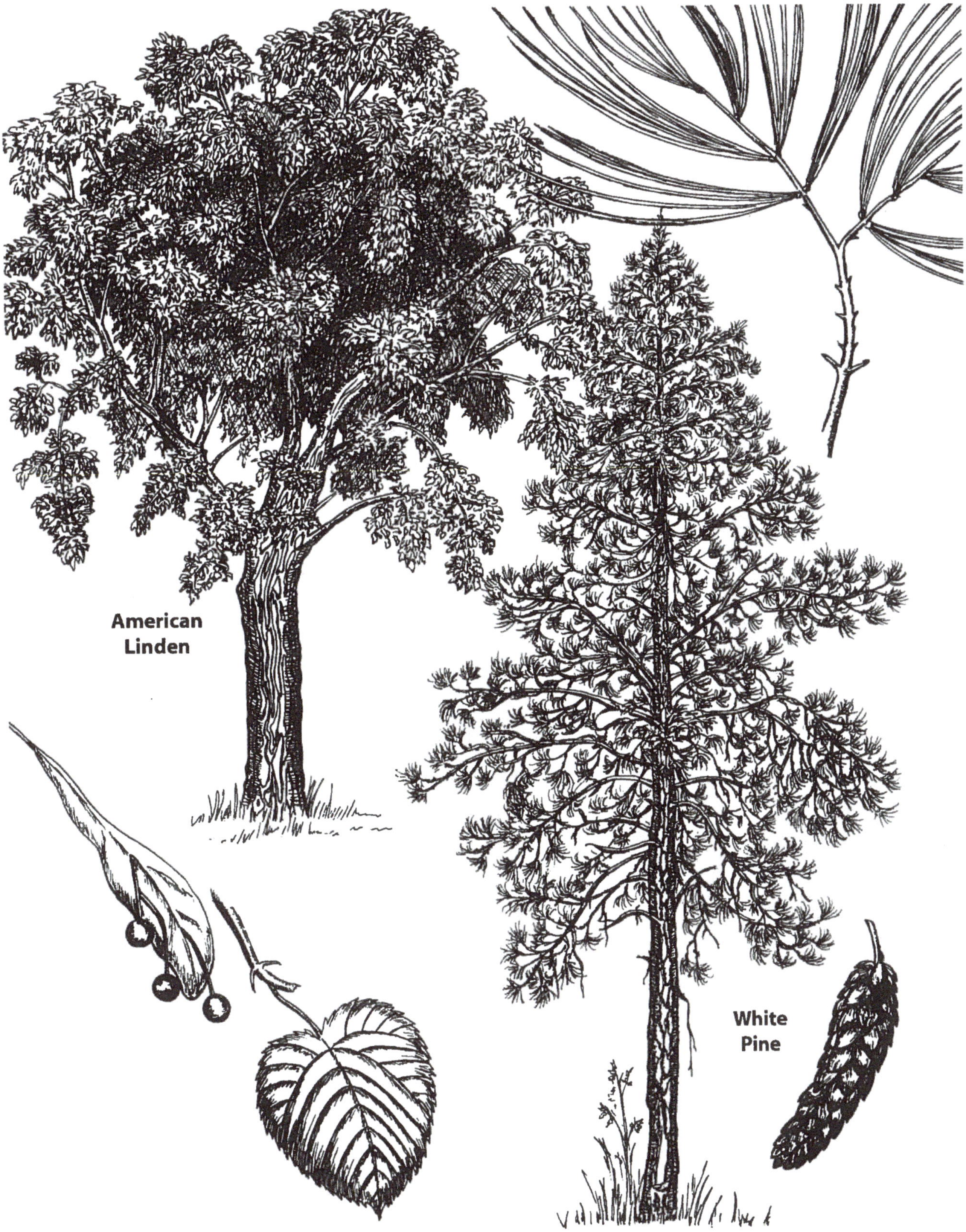

Coniferous & Deciduous Trees

American Linden

White Pine

33

# Green vs. Dry

The difference between a green tree and dry tree is life. The green living tree pictured here is a birch tree. Dry dead trees are called snags. When the wind blows, a green tree will bend with the wind. A dry tree will not, and if pushed too hard, will snap and topple.

In a similar way, when family members are full of the life and power of the resurrected Christ, the winds of conflict are unable to break them. Instead they bend, yet stay true, kind, and friendly. People without the indwelling power of Christ are like dead trees: they snap into rude and angry quarrels and are not fun to be around. But where there is life there is flexibility and joy. "He that hath the Son hath life. He that hath not the Son of God hath not life" (1 John 5:12).

When Jesus was on His way to the cross of Calvary to pay the penalty for our sins on a dead tree, women began to weep when they saw Him suffering. He thought of the future and said, "Then shall they begin to say to the mountains, Fall on us; and to the hills, Cover us. For if they do these things in a green tree, what shall be done in the dry?" (Luke 23:31 KJV).

By the green tree Jesus was speaking of Himself, the innocent Redeemer, being crucified for the sins of men. What suffering then would be borne by the dry tree, the sinner who continues in his sin?

Trees that are alive, die. Sometimes this death is senseless. "It took more than 3,000 years to make some of the trees in these western woods ... Through all the wonderful, eventful centuries since Christ's time...and long before that... God cared for these trees, saving them from drought, disease, avalanches, and a thousand straining, leveling, tempests and floods; but He cannot save them from fools." Taken from *The American Forest* by John Muir.

Man can take a living tree and make it dead. But man cannot take a dead tree and make it live. With what careful respect then should we take life from a tree when we cannot give its life back! One of the miracles of redemption is that a dry tree, a person dead in trespasses and sins, can accept Jesus Christ and allow Him to live in his heart, and thereby become as a living tree.

 PRACTICAL PROJECT

Take up some dry twigs and bend them; see how little pressure it takes before they snap. Do the same to a living twig; see how far it will bend before it breaks. Then discuss family relationships. How can we let the life of the living Jesus be revealed in our lives when family members may bend our patience to the breaking point?

Green vs. Dry

35

Growth

Out of every million seeds hanging on trees in autumn, perhaps only one will actually sprout. Even after receiving the gift of life, each tiny seedling still has many obstacles to surmount before it will become a mature tree.

Below ground, seedlings are attacked by insects such as cutworms. Above ground, armies of termites, blackwood ants and others, take their toll. Different insects are attracted by different species of trees. Squirrels, chipmunks and sparrows, all eye them as fresh green salad. Deer browse on them. If a seedling survives its first year, it has hope of decades, or even centuries, of further growth.

Children today experience some of the hazards of young saplings. Diseases and accidents take their toll. And in early childhood, some are crippled by lack of love and attention from father or mother. Fears and pressing needs may hide the sun of God's love from their view. Psalm 68:5 gives us this assuring promise, "He is a father to the fatherless."

In order for the tiny sapling to continue growing by the roots of its parent, its needs must be met. No growth takes place through any anxiety or power of its own. It grows not by trying but relying on what is provided. It lays hold on water and nourishment from the ground and absorbs the air and light from above.

So it is with children. Often the innocence of childhood has almost been wiped away by the glare of television and the roar of condominium living; but a most delightful promise for wise young sprigs is found in Jeremiah 17:7, 8: "Blessed is the man [boy or girl] who trusts in the Lord ... For he shall be like a tree planted by the waters, which spreads out its roots by the river, and will not fear when heat comes: But its leaf will be green, and will not be anxious in the year of drought, nor will cease from yielding fruit."

PRACTICAL PROJECT

Take a walk in the woods and note how many seedlings you can find in a given area.

Compare that to how many mature trees are growing in the same area.

With your parents or a teacher, make a list of the hazards of youth and childhood.

Which ones do we have any control over?

What promises can be found in scripture to secure growth, especially the growth that lasts eternally?

Find a promise for every hazard of youth.

Growth

Thinning

Near Polebridge, Montana, are many densely covered hillsides with trees 10 to 12 feet tall. Most of the trees are no bigger around than a donut, yet they have been growing for 15 to 20 years! These trees are called a "Dog's hair" forest. Why are they so small and stunted? Because they have never been thinned. These trees began to grow after a forest fire. When trees grow too close together there is not sufficient moisture or sunshine to grow well. Thoughtful lumbermen will thin a forest and, ideally, leave a variety of trees, some old, some young. The younger trees can grow, and they are protected with space.

In a similar way, God designed that each family would have a sacred circle that belongs only to that family. When we jam families into high-rise apartments we produce an overcrowded environment, resulting in an epidemic of crime and violence that is almost out of control in the cities. The words of Revelation 18:4 are appropriate: "Comer out of her, my people…lest you receive of her plagues." It would be good for families to prayerfully make plans to move to the countryside where there is space, quietness, and privacy, for God to speak to them.

Likewise, family members were not created to grow alike in the shadow of each other. Families need to give each member the space of privacy for developing his/her own individuality. Each has the power to think and do, and God desires them to have their own private relationship with Him. It would be contrary to nature for a father or mother to dominate children ruthlessly or for children to control their parents. "Don't let the world around you squeeze you into its own mould, but let God re-mould your minds from within" (Romans 12:2, Phillips).

In the parable of the sower in Luke 8, Jesus told how the good seed could bring no fruit to maturity because it was choked out by thorns and thistles. So we, with the power of God's Word, must thin our branches, removing music, books, videos and friends that do not leave enough time or space for the growth of His Word.

PRACTICAL PROJECT

Go for a walk in the woods and find where trees need thinning. In this environment, discuss if life in your family provides the space for warm loving relationships and room for each to grow differently according to the ability of each. Is there space for each to personally experience a loving relationship with Jesus?

Thinning

Forest Community

In this pictured forest are many different kinds of trees: cottonwood, lodgepole pine, cedar, birch, douglas fir, and ponderosa pine. They live together in a common neighborhood, each one differing slightly from the other and sharing the space, sunshine, and water to meet its own needs. They live together adapting to one another. One tree cannot be removed without affecting all the rest.

A study at Oregon State University found that when tree seedlings grow side by side, they are often joined by a type of fungus. If one seedling is in the shade and unable to get the sunlight it needs for survival, it can draw needed food and water from the bigger tree next door via their joined roots.

In the forest, contrary to what we have sometimes been taught, trees are not in competition with each other, but can form a cooperative network working together for survival. David Rhodes, chemical ecologist at the University of Washington, Seattle, was the first to discover that trees "communicate." They send unseen signals to each other. When tent caterpillars attack willows, the willow gives off a chemical that alerts nearby willows. These trees respond by pumping more tannin into their leaves, thus making their leaves more difficult for insects to digest.

At the bottom of the picture we see small fir trees growing in the sheltered protection of the parent tree. After centuries, the parent tree will die leaving room for the young trees to take its place. So it is with life. Parents will eventually die, and their children will live to carry on the family name. The forest community can be compared to the extended family, with great grandparents, grandparents, parents, and seedlings all growing together for centuries. "Teach my law diligently to your children and children's children" (Deuteronomy 6:6). Each member is a different personality with different needs. In spite of these differences, they work together helping one another.

In the sheltered environment provided by the extended family, children are brought up "In the nurture and admonition of the Lord" (Ephesians 6:4). After years of growing in this protected environment, one by one, the forefathers will step aside, allowing their children to pursue their goal of bringing glory to their Maker.

PRACTICAL PROJECT

Blindfold your children and take them off the trail into the forest, to a tree of your choosing. Let them examine the tree, while blindfolded—perhaps through smell as well as touch. Some trees have a peculiar fragrance. Then bring them back to the trail, take off the blindfold and let them find their tree. Then reverse this with the children leading the parent.

A family could plant a tree for each family member. Each child could have a certificate for their tree and could have a yearly photo taken with the tree—maybe on a birthday. As the tree and child grow together, they could help care for the tree.

Forest Community

Atmosphere

The atmosphere around a tree is invisible—yet very real! We become aware of its presence, as we feel the coolness in a tree's shade. This coolness is produced by its water atmosphere. Fact: An apple tree can evaporate four gallons of water, per hour, into its atmosphere. This atmosphere also contains oxygen made by leaves. When we breathe in deeply, we become aware of its refreshing, vitalizing oxygen. While oxygen cannot be seen, when you breathe in deeply in the out-of-doors you may become aware of a faint fragrance. This fragrance has a healing quality about it which is especially true of the eucalyptus tree. It opens up the air passages enabling us to breathe more freely.

In a similar way there is an atmosphere around your personal tree of life. While it cannot be seen, it is very real. Someone might say, "I don't like your attitude. I don't like your spirit. I don't like being around them." Why? There is an atmosphere around every individual just as real as the air you breathe. We do not come into its presence for very long before we can tell whether they are connected to Jesus or not.

In I Corinthians 10:31 it says, "Whatsoever you eat, drink or do, do all to the glory of God."

Your life may seem very small and insignificant. But if your life is rooted in God's Word, and you breathe out an atmosphere of His grace, your life will then fulfill the purpose of its Creator.Or, we may choose to root our lives in ourselves and become selfish. Then we create a negative vacuum around us that is very real.

I have noticed there is a compatibility of rebellion in some youth. You can travel hundreds of miles by bus with students to a new campus. In a few minutes of conversing, the rebellious students will join others that think the same. Conversely, the loyal, obedient students will gather together. They will be automatically attracted to that which attracts them. The old adage is, "Birds of a feather, flock together." Let us make our personal lives a tree of life, creating an atmosphere around us that will protect us from wrong friends and attract us to right friends.

 PRACTICAL PROJECT

Check out the atmosphere of a tree in hot sunshine. What do you feel in its shade? As your family visits other families, sense the invisible atmosphere around their homes. Then check out your own home. What is the atmosphere of your home? Is it loving, peaceful, and courteous? Or is it chilly with the gloom of grumbling, agitation, and selfish clamoring? The people in the family determine the atmosphere of their little forest home.

Atmosphere

43

Tree House

One of my fondest childhood memories is the Oak Tree Lodge where my brother and I slept every night one summer. As we lay down to sleep, the gentle rustle of the oak leaves and the distant singing of the Chuck-wills-widow, caused me to realize what a wonderful idea God had when He gave our first parents a garden home. It was their happy privilege to train the vines and trees into rooms. Perhaps the walls of their kitchen were fragrant with living fruit. Adam and Eve were to "tend and keep the garden" (Genesis 2:15).

Trees are home for many creatures. Woodpeckers drill in the tree trunk and tunnel downward, making a home up to one foot deep. Raccoons and opossums make their home in the hollow of a tree. "Even the sparrow has found a home, and the swallow a nest for herself, where she may lay her young" (Psalm 84:3). Squirrels nest in tree branches or in a hollow cavity. They don't have to travel far for food because they feed on the tender leaves or nuts. They have all this without paying rent or a grocery bill.

Trees act as a shelter in a storm—insects crawl in for shelter; raccoons and smaller animals climb trees for safety. We have watched bear cubs swaying at the top of a tree while their mother was up another tree with the neighbor's dog barking below.

Our homes are to be like the sheltering branches of a tree, a safe place for children to grow, protected by the branches of mother and father. "The eternal God is our refuge and underneath are the everlasting arms" (Deuteronomy 33:27).

Trees when cut down are sawed into lumber. The lumber is then used to build our homes. Trees are a fit symbol of a safe protected home.

PRACTICAL PROJECT

Look at one tree for an hour or two and record how many different creatures stop there, live there, or find shelter there.

Build memories for your children by building a tree house or a swing.

As a family, sit down and ponder if your home is a safe place. Ask the children if they feel safe there. Are there any areas of danger like air waves, video waves, wrong friends, or harmful food or drink set before them? Decide how you can make your home a godly tree of righteousness, safe for all, both family members and guests.

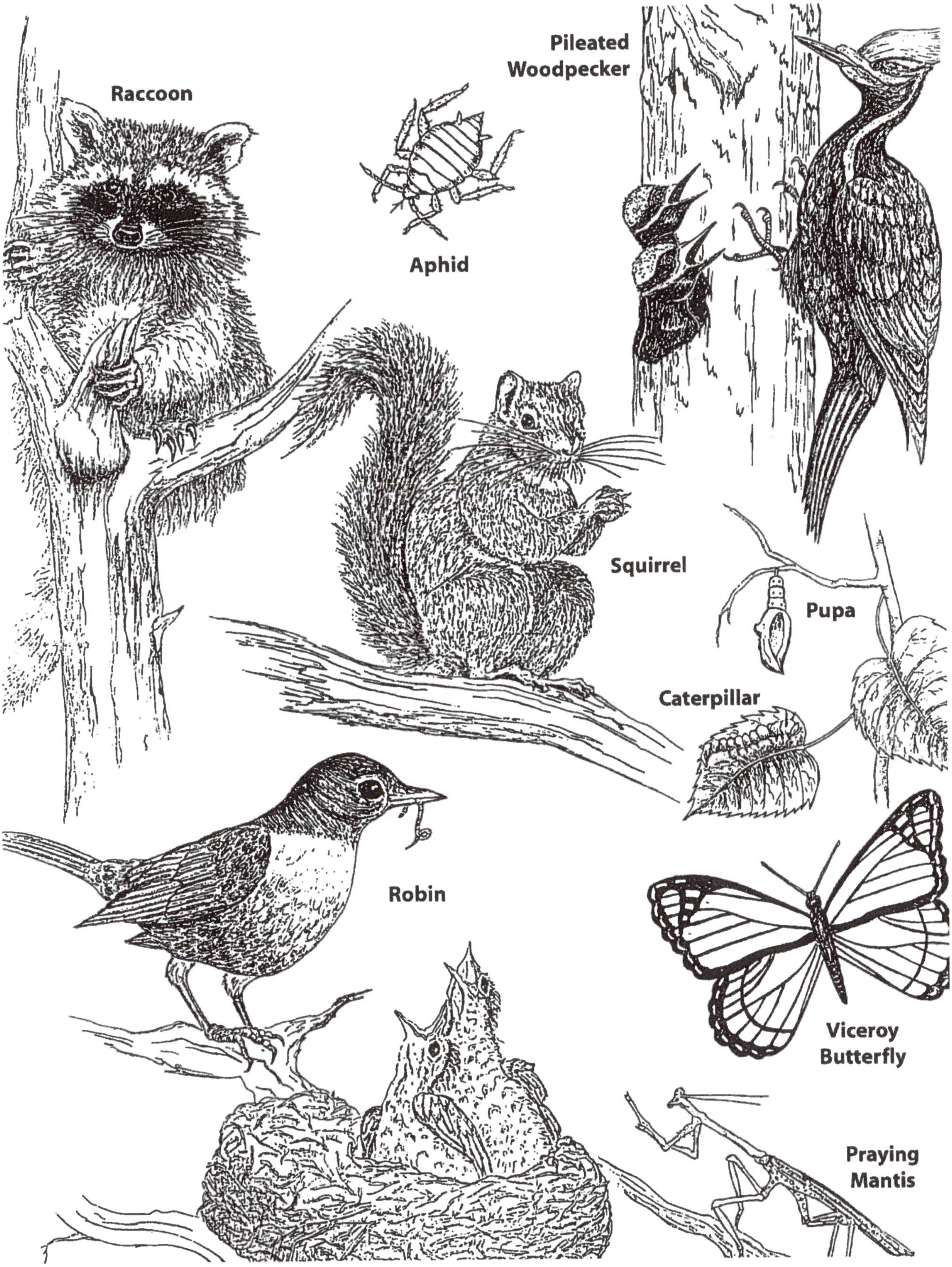
Raccoon
Aphid
Pileated
Woodpecker
Squirrel
Pupa
Caterpillar
Robin
Viceroy
Butterfly
Praying
Mantis

Tree Values

Trees are one of the most valuable living things for men. Someone counted 4,500 ways in which man uses the materials of a tree. One of the greatest uses of a tree that goes almost unnoticed, is its capacity to change carbon dioxide into carbohydrates. It also releases oxygen from its water intake. Although oxygen is invisible and silent, our life depends upon it.

Trees are an evidence of how much our Father in heaven cares for His children. He not only made the trees useful, but He also made them beautiful. The beauty of a tree, its gracefulness, its silent pointing from this earth to the sky, is a continual appeal for man to worship his Maker.

Another major use of a tree is its fruit. Fruit such as apples, oranges, and bananas, as well as nuts, are all so important in balancing the diet of a family. Jesus said, "Therefore, by their fruits you shall know them" (Matthew 7:20). In the same way, the fruits of a home are its children. Successful is that home whose children reflect their Maker.

The paper this book is printed on is made from wood pulp, which may come from any of the following: spruce, hemlock, southern pine, balsam, fir, cottonwood or aspen.

The most common use of a tree is what can be made with its wood. Around the world there may be as many as 100,000 species of trees. Each one has its own special qualities. When a tree is dead, its wood becomes useful. After the tree dies, the use and function of the wood will carry on for centuries. There are the rubber trees that produce rubber, pine trees that produce turpentine, cork trees whose bark becomes cork – the uses are almost endless.

God makes each tree for its own particular purpose, use and function, and so it is with people. God creates His children with potential skills, abilities, and talents for His specific purpose. He does not expect the cedar tree to have the functions or purposes He created the hyssop tree to perform.

And so, God gives members of the family their unique skills and abilities, beginning in the Mother's womb, according to Psalm 139. "You saw me when as yet there was an unformed substance." God has a purpose for the talents, abilities, and skills He gave you – a use that will result in honor and glory to your Creator and a blessing to your fellow man. Thank God for the gift of trees and thank God for creating you and me.

PRACTICAL PROJECT

Go through your home as a family and list every use of wood you can find. What special skills or talents has God given each member of your family?

Tree Values

Answers: 1. Table 2. Chair 3. Paper 4. Ruler 5. Wooden spoon 6. Fruit 7. Wooden bowl 8. Nuts 9. Book 10. Barrel 11. Wood for fireplace 12. Paneling 13. Fireplace top 14. Picture frame 15. Railroad ties 16. Car tires 17. Pencil

47

Tree Music

Trees make music. We often think of a tree making music when out of its wood is created an oboe, violin, or clarinet. There is a whole section in an orchestra called the woodwinds. But on this page, we are thinking of a different kind of tree music, one rarely heard.

When we bring to the study of trees the listening ear, we may hear this tree music being played on the tree limbs by the wind. In our noisy fast-paced world, learning to listen and hear what the breeze whispers through the limbs is almost a lost art. It is easy to walk through a beautiful forest setting so engrossed in our own thoughts that we scarcely hear the still small rustle of leaves.

On the opposite page is the leaf of the quaking aspen. This leaf is so delicately attached to the tree that the slightest whisper of a breeze will send the aspen leaves quaking, making their gentle "white noise" tunes. A breath of air can be so slight that it cannot even be felt, and yet that gentle breeze will set the leaf fluttering.

Jesus said the Holy Spirit blows where it will. Oh that our consciences were so in tune and in harmony with the will of God that at His slightest whisper we would move in perfect harmony with His desire or plan with no variance between what God says and what we think and do.

Trees of themselves are totally silent. They make no noise of themselves. It's the wind blowing on the tree that makes the music. In a similar way our human hearts are silent and bankrupt of any real love, but by the moving of the Holy Spirit, through God's Word, the human heart begins to sing music of heavenly origin—His unselfish love.

Perhaps God may reveal His will through rustling of the leaves, as God revealed His will to David through the sound of marching in the tops of the mulberry trees (see 2 Samuel 5:24). As we listen, blocking out all other sounds around us, the silence of the soul will make more distinct the voice of God.

God gave direction to David regarding how to fight a battle in 2 Samuel 5:23, 24. When he heard the wind blowing in the tops of the mulberry trees, he was to go forth. The Lord fought for them. May we learn to hear the Holy Spirit speaking in our hearts. He then can direct our lives, filled with the music of heaven.

PRACTICAL PROJECT

As a family, go for a walk in the woods, and sit down under a big tree. If the wind is blowing, close your eyes and listen. Count how many distinct melodies and tunes you can hear as the wind passes through the tree. Can you hear the trees of the field clapping their hands as Isaiah 55:12 pictures?

The leaves of a quaking Aspen swing back and forth in a slight breeze. This happens because the leaf petiole is flattened at right angles to the plane of the leaf blade. Try to examine this with a magnifying glass.

Petiole

In the Rain

Wherever rain falls there is abundant life. Rain forests receive some eighty inches per year and produce giant trees that grow over two hundred feet tall. Consider a normal forest in a gentle rain. Duck your head under the branches of a birch tree, while it rains.

Close your eyes and listen to the sound of the rain. Hear the sh-sh-sh-sh sound? That natural relaxing piece of music is called white sound. Each note is produced by a single drop of rain falling upon a single leaf. Like listening to rain, hearing kind words spoken, such as please, thank you, and may I, gladden the heart of a family.

With the eyes open, watch the drops land with a splat on the leaf. What does the leaf do? Bend? Can you hear the sound at the same time as rain hits the leaf?

As the rain falls, take a sniff and notice the forest perfume. The rain washes dust from the air, and little odors that are there all the time become dominant. The spicy fragrance of balsam and fir combine with birch and cedar to make an intoxicating elixir. The air is cool, yet not cold, and has an earthy smell, but not a dirty one. The air is fresh and vibrant with life.

"For as the rain comes down, and the snow from heaven, and do not return there, but water the earth ... So shall my word be that goes forth out of My mouth; it shall not return to Me void, but it shall accomplish what I please, and it shall prosper in the thing for which I sent it" (Isaiah 55:10, 11).

God wants to water our hearts with His Word like He does the world with rain. That Word received into our hearts will wash away the dust of selfishness, leaving us fragrant with His dynamic Life. With motives washed clean, we can perfume our world with the fragrance of His love.

 PRACTICAL PROJECT

As a family, with raincoats on, take a walk in the woods in a gentle rain. CAUTION: Not in a lightning and thunderstorm. Stand beneath the trees. Close your eyes and listen. Count the number of tunes that you hear. Count the number of odors that you smell. When the sun comes out after the storm, count the different colors in the little droplets that rest on the shiny tops of leaves. How many inches of courtesy did your family receive today?

In the Rain

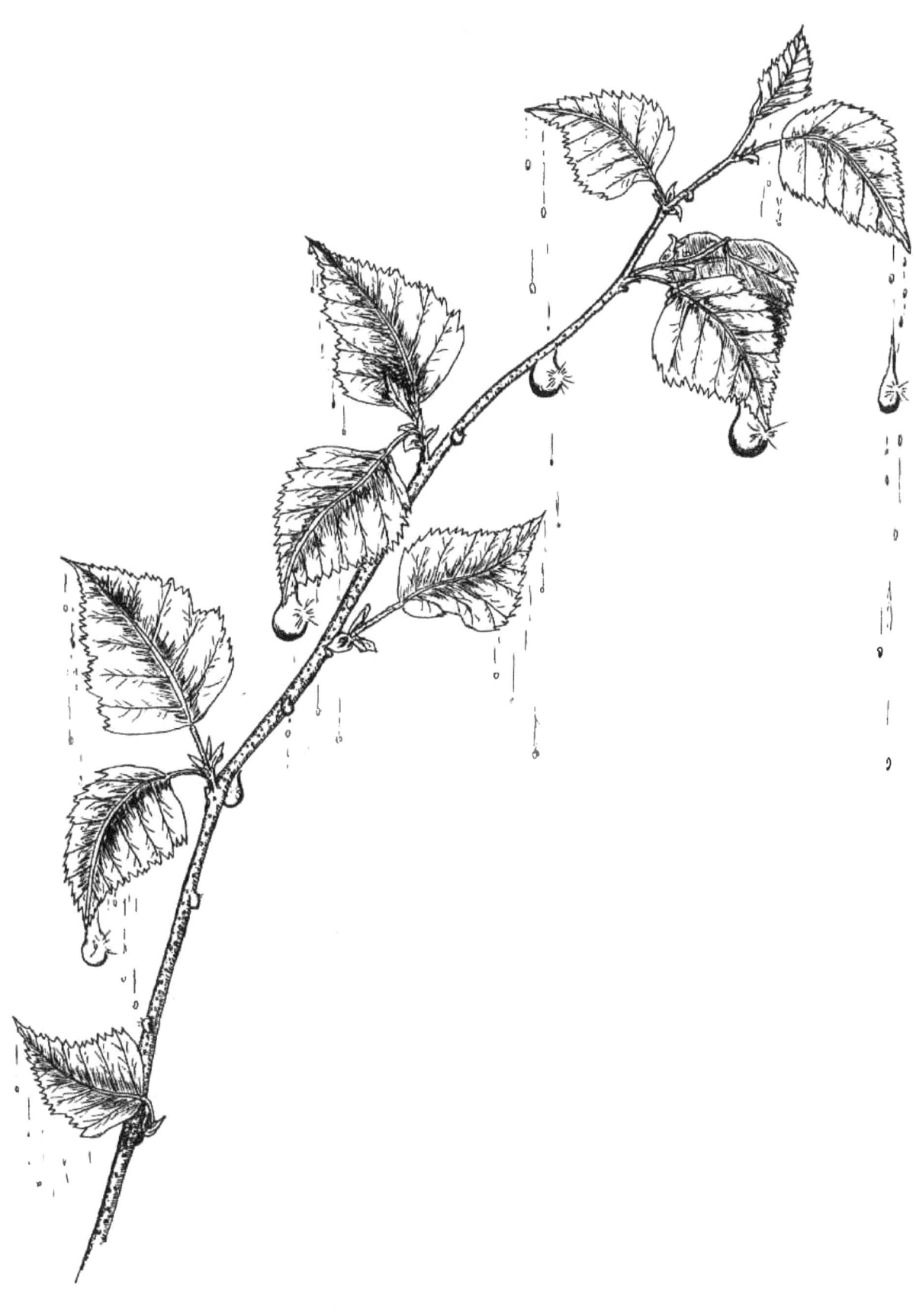

Tree Memories

Have you ever returned home after a long absence and viewed a cherished tree as if it were a long-lost friend? A thousand memories are recalled. Carved initials on the bark of the old tree and the rope marks on the branch where the swing once hung remind us of hours of delight. For many city children no such memories exist. They have concrete jungles, air and noise pollution and neighborhood fights.

Trees record history. By the Elster gate of Wittenberg, is a green oak tree. Under the limbs of this tree Luther took a stand for Scripture and helped rescue God's Holy Word from the Dark Ages. Under the shadow of the Oaks of Mamre, Abraham built an altar to God and beneath the branches of the same tree, held an interview with the angels. There, Abraham spoke with God as a man speaks with a friend. It was under the Olive branches that the Creator of this world, Jesus, decided the human fate in the Garden of Gethsemane when He prayed the victorious prayer, "not My will, but Yours, be done" (Luke 22:42).

In the Garden of Eden, when the evening breeze breathed upon leafy branches, our first parents would listen with breathless awe for the divine voice. Under trees the first church was conducted. That same voice that spoke in the Garden still speaks today.

Happy the family who still listens for that voice on the day God said was His. (See Exodus 20:8–11) They take their children and have a picnic beneath the branches, and there share Christ's parables in the setting in which they were given. Parents, let us build memories of God's ways beneath the trees. "Worship Him who made heaven and earth, the sea and springs of water" (Revelation 14:7).

PRACTICAL PROJECT

Jesus had an Olive Grove with memories, "He went to the Mount of Olives as He was accustomed" (Luke 22:39). Find a special tree or place, where you can meet regularly to commune with your Creator. Lead your children to find a special place in nature where they can commune alone with God.

Ask your parents about the important trees in their childhood—the trees upon which they climbed, trees where they hid, or trees around which they played.

Tree Memories

Cedar of Lebanon

Awesome in beauty, majestic in height, refreshing in its fragrance, the divine Creator has declared this tree king of the forest. The horizontal branches at the base of this tree are often wider than the tree is tall. The cedar is mentioned over 70 times in scriptures. This tree aptly illustrates God's desire for His people. "The righteous...shall grow like a cedar in Lebanon" (Psalm 92:12). It is His plan that the godly shall be beautiful, and their influence widespread.

The cedar tree flourishes beside a riverside or on a parched and thirsty mountainside. It withstands the fiercest winds. What a fitting symbol for God's people who were to "Go to all the world" (Matthew 28:20). Like the cedar, Christians are able to survive in just about any environment on this sinful earth. So, the Christian is to go to all the world and make disciples, reproducing the life of Christ in human clay.

The rose-shaped cone on this tree takes about two years to mature and looks very much like a rose. It is about four to five inches in length and two inches wide. It produces tiny seeds. Because of its lasting endurance this tree is valuable for its lumber and has been heavily logged, till very few are left.

Its wood is almost totally resistant to rot and decay, and insects rarely harm the cedar because of its very pungent protective odors.

Each family is to have all the enduring qualities of the cedar of Lebanon, making fragrant the home with heavenly graces.

We speak of our family tree and our roots. They ultimately end up back at God through Adam who was "the Son of God" (Luke 3:38). It was God's plan for the family tree, that there be a permanent one woman, one man love relationship, with children, as the wedding vow says, "as long as life shall last." Only being rooted and grounded in Christ can enable the modern home to grow like the cedar of Lebanon.

PRACTICAL PROJECT

Gather fresh pine or cedar needles. Squeeze or crush them and smell the aroma. Note the effect on lungs and breathing. Is it a pleasant smell?

When our rights are squeezed or crushed, what aroma do we share? Is it the perfume of a meek and quiet spirit of Jesus, in harmony with the Ten Commandments? Or is it the stench of "BO," a "tit for tat" and selfishness?

Cedar of Lebanon

Tree of Good & Evil

According to Genesis 2:9, 16, 17, this ancient tree of good and evil once grew in the midst of the Garden of Eden. At that time all you could see was beauty all over the tree. It looked like a good tree, and it seemed a good tree. Proverbs says, "there is a way that seems right, but ends in death" (Proverbs 14:12).

God forbid man to partake of this tree of knowledge of good and evil. It was never in God's plan of love for man to know evil, yet man must have freedom to choose. Trusting in the words of the serpent Adam and Even partook of the tree that God had forbidden, thus surrendering their will to the serpent. The goal to be their own final authority resulted in selfishness taking the place of love. Thus, the human race became a slave of Satan.

The seeds of this tree are still bearing their fruit in our world today. One of the most fruitful trees of good and evil is television, movies, and DVDs. Satan's best fruit on this tree is a movie 90% good with only 10% evil. The evil invades the mind mixed with good. Gradually the mix is changed to 80% good and 20% evil, until finally we are watching 10% good and 90% evil. By beholding we are changed and lose the ability to know good from evil. (See Galatians 6:7–9.)

In Scriptures we read the words, "A good tree cannot bear bad fruit, nor can a bad tree bear good fruit ... Therefore by their fruits you shall know them" (Matthew 7:20). Other sources of mixed seeds are found in music, books, magazines, videos, and computer games. All are avenues to the soul: seeing, hearing, touching, tasting, and smelling.

Our only safety today is to avoid the tree with the mix of good and evil. We should stay as far from it as possible. Evil is found appealing in the future tense, never in the past tense. Drinking might appear fun until there is a hangover and the money is spent. Smoking appears to be fun until there is lung cancer, not to count the lost money. Evil is joy only in anticipation, never in the past tense. We should guard the avenues of our souls so none of the seed of this tree can find lodging in our hearts.

Fungus, stingers, thorns, sickness, and death are the visible fruits of the tree of good and evil. God never wanted us to know pain and death. Vera, the artist of this book, never finished this picture because cancer cut short her life.

PRACTICAL PROJECT

On a nature walk, look for evil fruits of this tree—thorns, thistles, stingers, insect pests etc.... Make a list. What would life without them be like? As a family do a search of your home to see if there are any seeds of this deadly tree growing there, and then uproot them by claiming the promise, "For me and my house, we will serve the Lord" (Joshua 24:15). Use Philippians 4:8 as a divine filter for everything coming into your home. Place this text right in the middle of your entertainment center.

Tree of Good & Evil

57

Wounds & Diseases

When your finger is cut, and red blood begins to spurt forth, you cry out in alarm. After you clean it and put a band-aid on, it feels better. Mother had something all prepared before you were hurt. All nature reveals this love that heals and restores. Notice the way a tree responds when it is hurt.

Trees have enemies. Some are listed on the opposite picture. One enemy, a beetle, bores holes in the bark. Once the bark is broken, it can eat little tunnels in the tree. These tunnels allow fungus spores to enter and eat away the life of the tree from the inside. Moisture also enters, causing the wood to begin to rot and bacteria to grow. In time the tree is destroyed. We are like these enemies when we carelessly cut a tree with an ax or knife.

In a similar way, we can let into our minds improper thoughts through things we look at, listen to, and do. Once entry is made, lies begin making tunnels of rottenness from the inside out, which will eventually destroy us.

When a tree is cut, sap immediately flows to the wound, like blood does when we are cut. There it thickens and turns into a gooey substance, closing up the wound, keeping out fungus, spores, moisture and bacteria. When a tree is young and healthy, sap can flow so fast that an insect can't even get inside the tree, because the sap keeps pushing him out. When the sap is not flowing fast, the insect can get inside and do its damage. By weeping it is healed.

I saw a tree once that was bound by a fence wire. The tree could not break the wire and so it grew all around it and over it, leaving hardly a mark, with just a piece of wire sticking out. So it is with childhood hurts and wounds. They will not destroy our happiness or usefulness when we make use of God's healing remedies. "Bless the Lord Oh my soul ... who forgives all your iniquities and heals all your diseases" (Psalm 103:2, 3).

Before sin arose, there was a healing remedy ready in Jesus. At the cross He paid the penalty for all the sins of this world, including yours and mine. He tasted the very depths of all that is black and ugly and painful, that He could sympathize with us in our sufferings. "By His stripes we are healed" (Isaiah 53:5). When we realize that He has experienced our pain, plus much more, we find in Him a true friend and comforter. His understanding love touches our innermost soul, cleansing and healing us of our sins and the sins of our forefathers.

PRACTICAL PROJECT

Look at a wounded tree. Can you see the healing agencies at work? What healing agencies have you allowed to work in your life? Can you become part of the healing team as is revealed in all nature? First receive healing yourself, then you are prepared to help a wounded friend find healing.

Wounds & Diseases

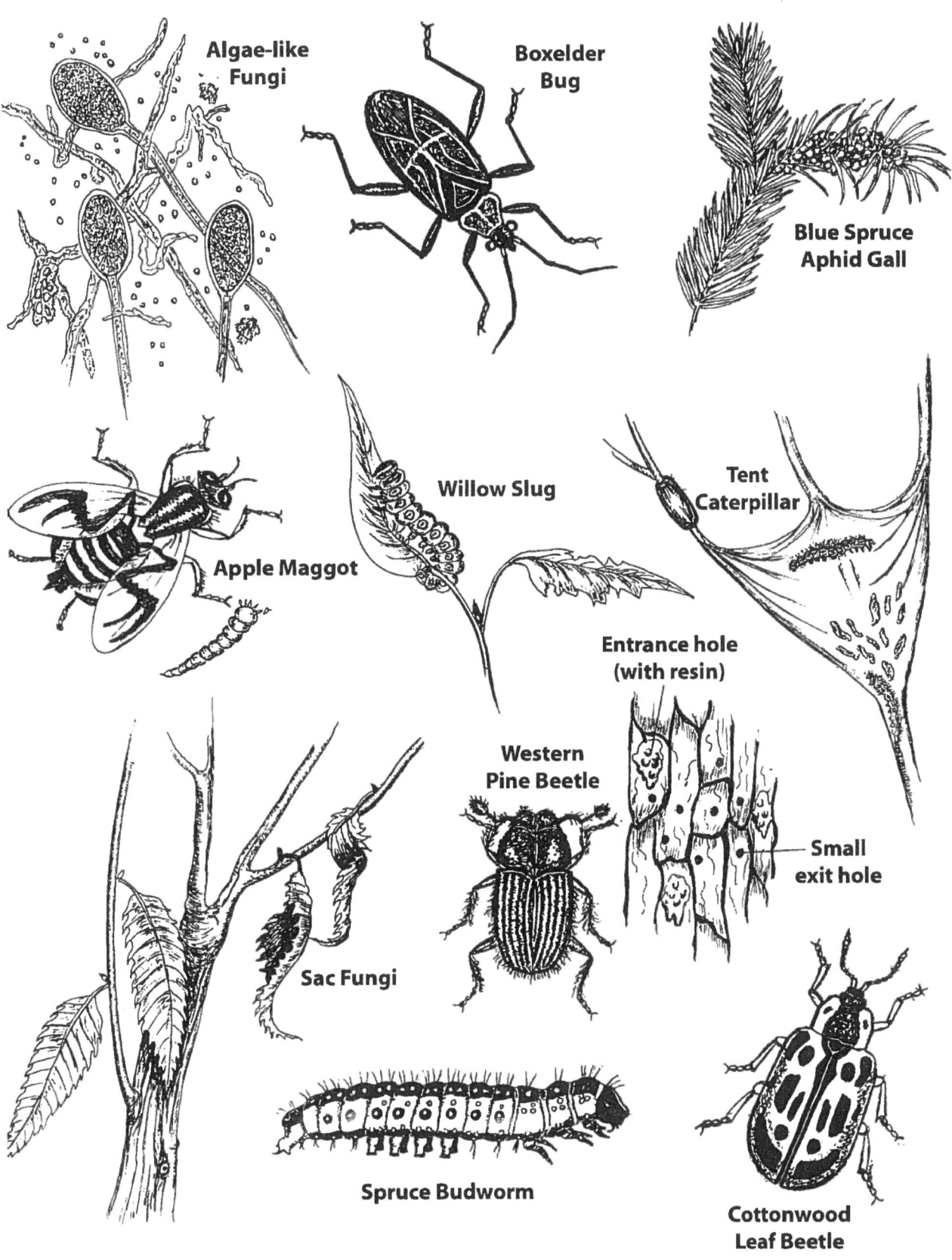

Death of a Tree

We grieve seeing a mighty forest giant, lying mute upon the ground. This former living tower—dead. An enemy has done this. God never wanted death in our world. "The wages of sin is death" (Romans 6:23). The fruit of Adam and Even's sin is "For dust you are, and to dust you shall return" (Genesis 3:19). Our Creator takes this curse—death—and makes it an essential part of God's recovery plan.

During growing years, a tree absorbs large amounts of water, nutrients, and minerals from earth. These, processed by leaves, and energy from the sun, are stored inside the tree. After death these stored treasures return to earth. Thus, its life's collection of blessings are given as a legacy to future generations. "Blessed are the dead who die in the Lord from now on... that they may rest from their labors, and their works do follow them" (Revelation 14:13). Decay recycles past stored energy for future saplings.

Trees die slowly, often requiring centuries of time. Tree bark resists insect damage and disease, but freezing, thawing, and prolonged dampness, weaken the bark. Microscopic bacteria and fungi sneak through the bark and soften the heartwood. Next come tunneling insects, beetles, wood wasps, larva, termites, and carpenter ants. Eventually this tree becomes so weakened from the inside out, it can no longer hold up its own weight and crashes to the ground.

Earth then becomes a funeral parlor for the tree, with the Creator's million undertakers completing the change. Shell fungi, mosses, and mushrooms, weaken the remains. Millions of earth worms, wood-boring grubs and termites chew the wood into fine bits. Bacteria finish the burial "from dust thou art and to dust shalt thou return" (Genesis 3:19). A tree returns its life-time collection to the soil for future generations.

For parents to pass a lasting legacy to their children, death to sin is needed – a death to selfish desires. God has one remedy for sin – death. The Creator could create only one way to save our sin ravaged world—the cross—the death of His own Son. Death, the fruit of sin, is God's answer to the sin question—sin must die. "Reckon yourselves to be dead indeed to sin, but alive to God in Christ Jesus our Lord" (Romans 6:11). Jesus died, paying our penalty so the hoarded love of eternity, could make divine life available to every child of Adam. God "so loved" He "gave."

PRACTICAL PROJECT

Take a walk where you find a large tree that has fallen and is decaying. Look under the bark. See how many different insects and plants and fungi you find growing there. Think how God has taken something bad and made it a way of life for His many creatures.

Death of a Tree

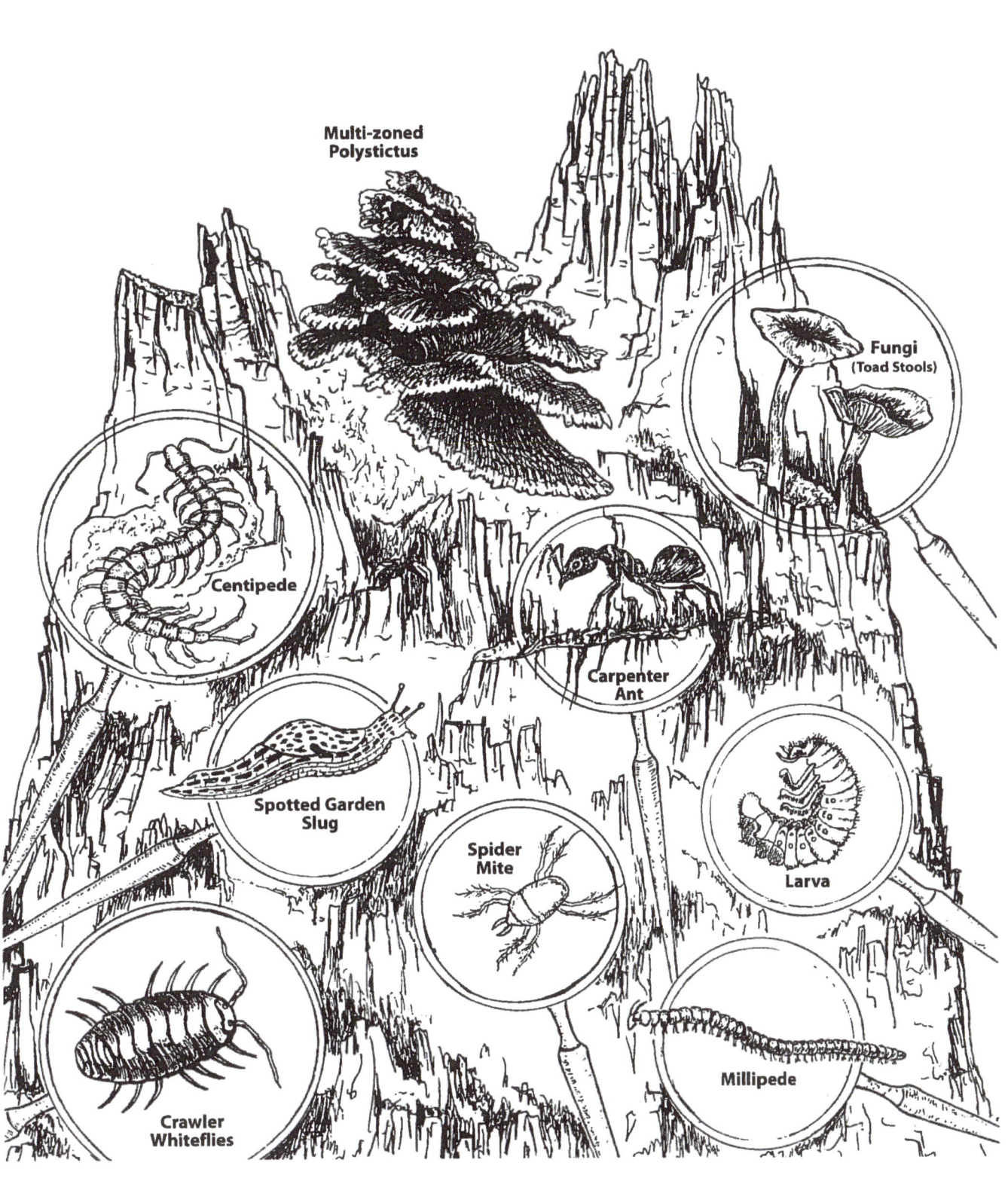

Four Seasons

Why does weather change from hot to cold? Summer to winter? Scientists tell us the seasons result from the tilt of the earth as it travels its yearly elliptical journey around the sun. But who tilts the earth? Why at an exact angle? How does the earth know to follow an elliptical journey around the sun? Why not a circle?

Who designed deciduous trees to put on its spring coat of buds, summer coat of green, fall coat of yellows and reds, or winter its coat of ice and snow? Each one of these different coats involves a very complex, complicated change, and each change depends upon another change having taken place just before it. "Blessed be the name of God forever and ever, for wisdom and might are His, and He changeth the time and the seasons" (Daniel 2:21). It is God who has tilted the earth and keeps it at that precise angle and guides it on its unseen journey around the sun.

The lengthening days of spring stimulate the trees' growth hormones along with an incredible release of stored energy. The tree uses most of this stored energy to produce new leaves, twigs, and wood. How wonderfully thoughtful it was for the tree to practice self-denial last summer and save some of its excess energy for the next spring. It did not squander its summer away in riotous living, as did the prodigal son. (See Luke 15:11–32.)

Seasons of a tree are a fit symbol of the seasons of human life. The bud stage of young childhood, bursting forth with new life. The leaf stage of summer with its maturing growth and seed production. The fall of the year as it loses abilities it once had, and then the grave of winter, a time for sleeping.

At each season, the tree is preparing for the next season. This whole seasonal change is not luck or chance, but rather that of some incredible mysterious timing. The seasons never take a tree by surprise. The tree practices self-denial at every stage in preparation for the next season. It pours its best into seed—for the generation to come. "Remember now your Creator in the days of your youth, before the difficult days come, and the years draw near when you say, 'I have no pleasure in them'" (Ecclesiastes 12:1).

To live in harmony with the Creator's ongoing commands during the bud stage of childhood requires a self-denial such as seen in the trees. "My son, hear the instruction of your father, and do not forsake the law of your mother" (Proverbs 1:8).

PRACTICAL PROJECT

Pick a particular deciduous tree or clump of deciduous trees consisting of birches, maples, or oaks. Mark on a calendar the four distinct seasons. Photograph it, sketch it, note the changes, and then talk about how the tree provides for the future season. How does this compare to our lives?

Four Seasons

63

Tree of Life

The most amazing tree that ever grew on earth is the tree of life (See Genesis 2:9). It possesses supernatural power. To eat of this tree is to live forever. Imagine the flavor and the vigor its fruit contains. God gave it the power to perpetuate life. Man did not receive immortality in the beginning. It was conditional upon obeying God and continuing to eat of this incredible tree.

When our first parents sinned, God's first act was to remove from man this tree of life, "lest he put out his hand and take also of the tree of life, and eat, and live forever, therefore the Lord God sent him out of the Garden of Eden ... and He placed Cherubim (angels) at the east of the Garden of Eden, and a flaming sword which turned every way to guard the way to the tree of life" (Genesis 3:22–24).

Sometime before the flood God must have transferred the Garden of Eden to heaven because in the description of heaven in Revelation 22:1, 2 we read, "He showed me a pure river of water of life, clear as crystal, proceeding from the throne of God and of the Lamb. In the middle of its street, and on either side of the river, was the tree of life, which bore twelve fruits, and each tree yielding its fruit every month. The leaves of the tree were for the healing of the nations."

From our family tree of life, we can trace our ancestors back to Adam and Eve. Because they partook of the tree of knowledge of good and evil, death has been passed on to every generation. But the way to the tree of life and immortality is still available through Jesus Christ, by "exceeding great and precious promises that by these we might be partakers of the divine nature" (2 Peter 1:4). Promises of the Bible are as leaves of this amazing Tree. Studying and living by God's Word is the way we now eat the leaves of the tree of life. Revelation 2:7 says, "To him who overcomes I will give to eat from the tree of life, which is in the midst of the Paradise of God."

Overcomers again will eat from the same tree Adam and Eve once ate. "Blessed are those who do His commandments, that they may have the right to eat of the tree of life" (Revelation 22:14). There will be a different fruit every month. Its leaves heal all nations of the redeemed. The power of this fruit will impart vigorous life that will never end.

Once again, we study nature as Adam and Eve. Angels will be our companions and Jesus our teacher. There He will explain to us His gospel according to a tree.

PRACTICAL PROJECT

Draw a family tree of life. The fruit on this tree could be pictures of grandparents, uncles, aunts, and cousins. The leaves on this tree could be Bible promises that you claim for that family. Then photocopy and give them as Christmas or birthday presents.

Tree of Life

Appendix A—McComb Theory of Sap Movement Up A Tree by David and Terry McComb

In summer of 1988 David D. McComb began researching Engelmann spruce (*Picea engelmannii* Parry) xylem cells using the electron microscope at the University of Calgary. As a result of these studies we propose the following McComb theory of how sap goes up a tree.

These xylem cells reveal concave and convex dishes up the vertical sides of the cells. Both types of dishes have a small circular hole in the center. The cells are very long and overlap each other approximately half way (see figure A). The concave and convex dishes line up from one cell to the next. Sap flows from one cell to the next through these small holes.

We believe that there is a small membrane between the two xylem cells that is solid in the center and perforated or slotted on the edges. The orientation of the convex and concave dishes permits sap to flow in one direction but not the other direction.

The bottom half of the xylem cells have concave dishes and the top half of the cell have convex dishes. This would allow sap to flow into the bottom half of the cell and out the top half of the cell. This would function very much like the one-way valves that operate in the human blood vein. Blood flows up by muscular action, the valve retaining blood from flowing backwards.

Ray cells of a tree have always been somewhat of a mystery as to what their function is to a tree. Ray cells contain a nucleus, which could function by nervous-electro-impulse (See figure B). For the tree, the muscular constriction would be applied by the ray cells, which grow horizontal to the vertical xylem cells. The ray cells could be stimulated by the tree to make a minute constriction, just enough to cause sap to be moved to the next cell upward against the pull of gravity.

Another possibility could be that the ray cells absorb water and thus expand like a balloon, forcing the xylem cells to expel their sap and release water causing the adjacent xylem cells to pull more sap from the cells below. Either way the ray cells are expanding and contracting, causing the pumping action that forces sap up the tree trunk.

These constrictions of the ray cells would sweep up the tree in a rhythmical fashion. It would function like milking a cow's udder upward instead of downward. This pumping action could lift water to any height with very little effort. This could explain how sap goes up a 300-foot tall redwood tree. It would also explain how sap goes up a leafless maple tree in the cold of spring.

It is our belief that the tissue membrane that is between the two circle openings of adjacent xylem cells is destroyed in the process of preparing the specimens for the electron microscope. Further testing will be needed to prove this theory. How the nerve impulses are transmitted to the ray cell is unknown.

The more one searches into the secrets of the creation, the more one realizes the ignorance of man. Truly we are "fearfully and wonderfully made" (Psalm 139:14).

Appendix A

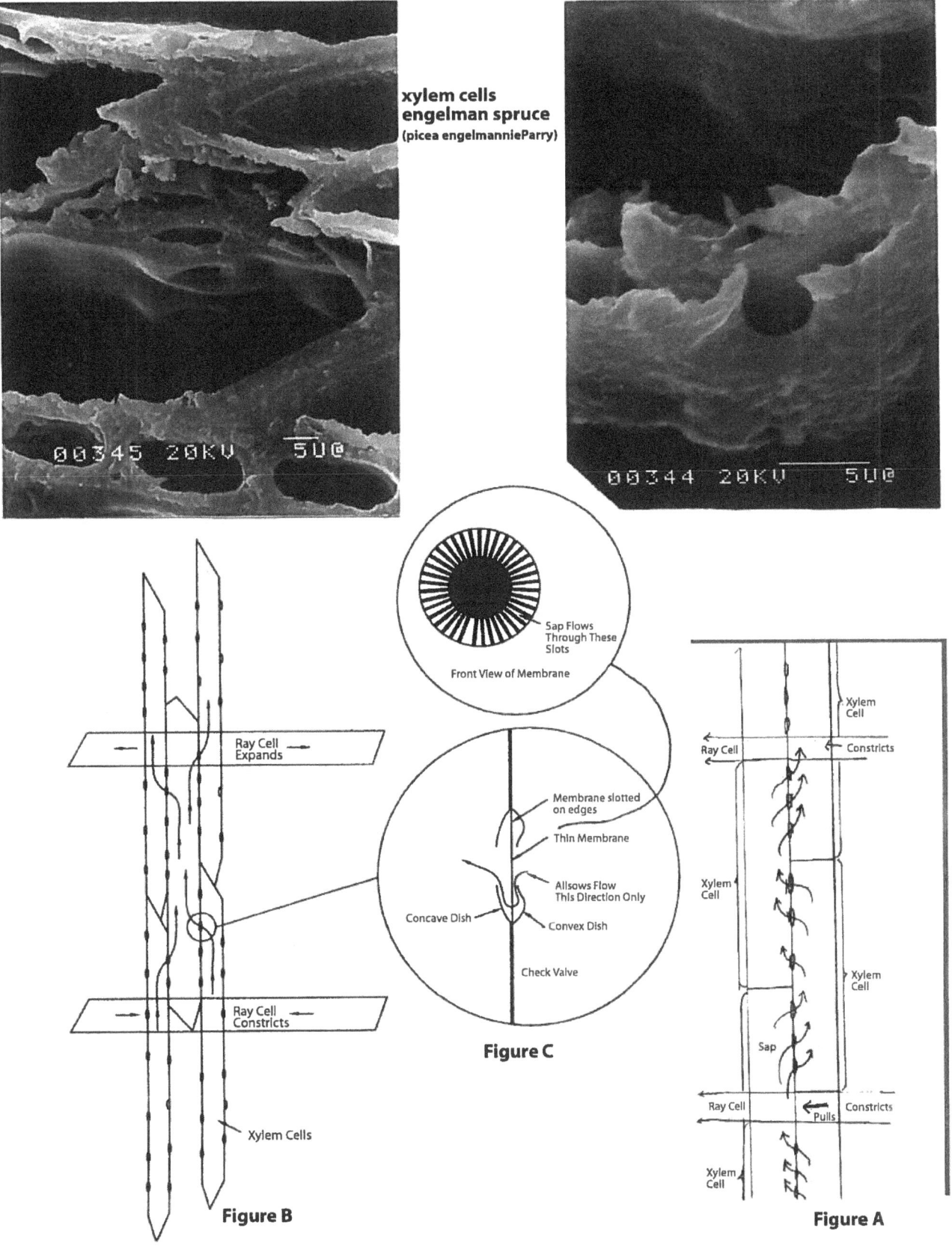

Bibliography

Anderson, D. *All the Trees and Woody Plants of the Bible*. Word, Inc. 1979.

Brown, W. *In The Beginning: Compelling Evidence for Creation and the Flood*. Center for Scientific Creation, 1995.

Cady, M. *Bible Nature Studies*. Pacific Press Publishing Company, 1901.

———. *The Education that Educates*. Fleming H. Revell Company, 1937.

Collingwood, G., and Brush W. *Knowing Your Trees*. The American Forestry Association, 1964.

Comstock, A. *Handbook of Nature Study*. University Press, 1939.

Graham, K., Hicks, L., Shimmin, D., and Thompson, G. *Biology God's Living Creation*. A Beka Book Publications, 1986.

Guinness, A. *Joy of Nature: How to Observe and Appreciate*. The Readers Digest Association, Inc. 1977.

Horan, A., and Mason R. *Trees: The Time-Life Gardener's Guide*. Time-Life Books, Inc.

Ingram, B. *Character Craft, per se: A Source Book in Moral Education*. Dupli-Craft Company Publishers, 1979.

Irving, H. *How to Know the Trees*. Cassell and Company, LTD, 1910.

Keller, P. *As a Tree Grows*. Fleming H. Revell Company, 1966.

Lewis, P. *40 Ways to Teach Your Child Values*. Tyndale House Publishers Inc., 1985.

March, D. *OUR FATHER'S HOUSE The Unwritten Word*. Ziegler & McCurdy, 1869.

McCormick, J. *The Life of the Forest*. McGraw-Hill Book Company, 1966.

Morris, H. *Science and the Bible*. Ziegler & McCurdy, 1873.

Our Amazing World of Nature—Its Marvels & Mysteries. The Readers Digest, Inc., 1969.

Peattie, D. *The Rainbow Book of Nature*. The World Publishing Company, 1957.

Platt, R. *This Green World*. Dodd, Mead & Company, 1945.

Spalding, A.W. *Love's Way, Life and Its Beginnings*. Pacific Press Publishing Association, 1976.

Walker, L. *Trees: An Introduction to Trees and Forest Ecology for the Amateur Naturalist*. A Spectrum book, Prentice-Hall, Inc., 1984.

Subscribe to the Leading Bible-based Nature Journal!

Readers call it, "The Christian answer to *National Geographic!*"

- Stunning Photography
- Animal & Bird Features
- Creation Science
- Outdoor Travel Adventures
- Gardening Tips
- Youth Photo & Coloring Contests
- Character-building Lessons found in Nature
- Instructional Study Guide
- Even Genesis Cuisine Recipes for healthful living!

UNPLUG and Get Away to Nature & Creation!

4 Quarterly Issues Only $19.95/year–INCLUDES a FREE Digital Subscription
ORDER NOW!

Logon to: **www.CreationIllustrated.com** or Call: **1(800) 360-2732**
or Mail a Check to: **Creation Illustrated, PO Box 141103, Spokane Valley, WA 99214**

The Gospel According to Creation Seminars

Terry McComb, Speaker and Writer with *Creation Illustrated* magazine, has conducted countless character-building, Bible-based seminars that reveal eternal truths through the handiwork of God. The Spiritual messages have a lasting impact on all ages and include blacklight chalk drawings with his wife's soft piano artistry in the background.

Pastor McComb has authored more than 50 articles with *Creation Illustrated* magazine and co-authored with his wife Jean, five children's books for parents to study with their children—*Gospel According to a Dandelion; Gospel According to a Blade of Grass; Gospel According to a Snowflake; Gospel According to a Thornless Blackberry;* and *Gospel According to a Tree.*

Available Seminars (available for purchase as a digital download or DVD copy):

"The Creation Story" is a scientific walk through Genesis one. How does each day of the Creation Week reveal its Author and how is this truth relevant to our spiritual walk? A nine-hour seminar from Sunday through Saturday night.

"In His Image" focuses on the wonder of the human body! This nine-hour seminar is a fast-moving study that examines the 12 systems of the body and their amazing designer. Deeply scientific, yet spiritual.

"The Wonder of a Tree" is a nine-hour seminar illustrating how the lifestyle, function, and ways of a tree reveal the ways of its Creator, Jesus Christ.

"Creations Creator" is a five-hour week-end seminar that addresses evolution vs. creation and the truth about Dinosaurs. Topics include: The Cross as Seen in Nature, Worship Him Who Made, Heart Reading Nature, and the Gospel According to a Dandelion power point presentation with music background.

"How to Heart Read Nature" will help viewers learn how to see past the trees and see the Creator. This is a hands-on practical nine-hour seminar that uses the out-of-doors classroom and needs to be in a nature setting. Short on theory and long on active learning.

"The Heavens are Telling" deals with The Gospel According to Astronomy" with plenty of NASA space telescope photos. This nine-hour seminar shows God's ways in outer space to help fill your heart's inner space with His love.

These Seminars can be done by Zoom
To Book a Seminar or order books and DVD's
Call: (250) 547-6696
E-mail: terry@gospelcreation.com
Web site: www.gospelcreation.com
Write: The Gospel According to Creation Seminar
39 Pine Road, Cherryville, British Columbia, Canada V0E 2G3

TEACH Services, Inc.
PUBLISHING

We invite you to view the complete
selection of titles we publish at:
www.TEACHServices.com

We encourage you to write us
with your thoughts about this,
or any other book we publish at:
info@TEACHServices.com

TEACH Services' titles may be purchased in
bulk quantities for educational, fund-raising,
business, or promotional use.
bulksales@TEACHServices.com

Finally, if you are interested in seeing
your own book in print, please contact us at:
publishing@TEACHServices.com

We are happy to review your manuscript at no charge.

www.ingramcontent.com/pod-product-compliance
Lightning Source LLC
Chambersburg PA
CBHW061604170426
43196CB00039B/2968